After the Cure

After the Cure

The Untold Stories of Breast Cancer Survivors

Emily K. Abel and Saskia Subramanian

Foreword by Patricia A. Ganz

NEW YORK UNIVERSITY PRESS
New York and London

7476

KH

NEW YORK UNIVERSITY PRESS
New York and London
www.nyupress.org

Library of Congress Cataloging-in-Publication Data

Abel, Emily K.
After the cure : the untold stories of breast cancer survivors /
Emily K. Abel and Saskia K. Subramanian.
p. cm.
Includes bibliographical references and index.
ISBN–13: 978–0–8147–0725–8 (cl : alk. paper)
ISBN–10: 0–8147–0725–4 (cl : alk. paper)
1. Breast—Cancer—Treatment—Complications. 2. Breast—Cancer—Psychological
aspects. 3. Antineoplastic agents—Side effects. I. Subramanian, Saskia K. II. Title.
RC280.B8A22   2008
616.99'449061—dc22   2008020941

New York University Press books are printed on acid-free paper, and
their binding materials are chosen for strength and durability. We strive
to use environmentally responsible suppliers and materials to the greatest
extent possible in publishing our books.

Manufactured in the United States of America

c   10 9 8 7 6 5 4 3 2 1
p   10 9 8 7 6 5 4 3 2 1

6|5|19

Contents

Acknowledgments

FIRST AND FOREMOST, we thank the women who opened their homes and their lives to us. The courage and thoughtfulness they demonstrated at every turn were humbling. The generous support from the Susan G. Komen Foundation also was critical to this study.

Rebecca Crane-Okada provided enormous assistance while we were developing and conducting the research. Other key members of the research team included Jean Cadigan, Judy Olweny, and Lotte Thomsen, as well as project managers Teresa Magula, Ana Johnson, and Kiavash Nikkhou. Many students completed the least glamorous but most crucial jobs such as data entry, coding, transcribing, and photocopying literature. Most notable for their longevity with the project are Nelli Boykoff, Kristina Contreras, Jennifer Johnson, Nicole Lee, Tasneem Motala, Georgia Scheele, and Jared Wong.

Rick Abel, Kathy Davis, Patricia Ganz, Janet Golden, Ilene Kalish, Rose Weitz, and two anonymous reviewers read the manuscript and offered wonderfully helpful advice. Margaret K. Nelson provided ongoing assistance about sociological methods.

Saskia also thanks her research mentor, M. Belinda Tucker, for providing guidance during this study. Saskia's late mother, Cornelia Termeulen, offered valuable assistance in crafting the Komen grant application, as well as loving moral and intellectual support. Her husband, Marcus Linden, proved a superb sounding board and was of great help at a number of junctures during the project.

Emily Abel thanks four doctors who provided models of care and compassion, Nancy Feldman, Patricia Ganz, Lois Schwartz, and Susan Stangl, as well as the many family and friends who offered crucial support both during cancer treatment and beyond.

Foreword

DURING THE SPAN of my career in medicine, breast cancer has been transformed from a disease that was hidden from family and friends to one that has a public face with a strong advocacy movement. Most women and men have familiarity with the diagnosis and treatment of breast cancer based on frequent newspaper and magazine articles, including descriptions of the medical treatment of high-profile celebrities and public figures. Less well-known are some of the difficulties faced by women who have been treated for breast cancer. In this volume, the authors provide an in-depth exploration of the symptoms experienced by some women after breast cancer treatment, giving voice to a neglected aspect of the breast cancer experience. As Drs. Abel and Subramanian point out in their introduction, breast cancer is now a chronic disease (as are most other cancers after curative intent treatment), mostly due to the success of multimodal therapies that may lead to long-term persistent symptoms. In addition, the fear of distant recurrence and the required surveillance for second cancers in the breast heighten a woman's anxiety and increase awareness of her vulnerability. Life was much simpler in some ways for the breast cancer patient fifty years ago, when after a radical mastectomy, she was told by her surgeon, "I got it all!" In fact, the survival rate then was about half what it is today.

There is certainly a high price to pay for increased survival resulting from contemporary cancer therapy. Breast cancer treatments are complex, toxic, and costly, and they take many months to complete. There is a toll on families and relationships during this time, and when treatment ends, the woman is faced (often alone) with putting her life back on track. Family members, friends, and the medical staff may wish to celebrate the milestone of the completion of treatment, but the breast cancer patient knows that for her, life will never be the same. Nevertheless, many women are extremely resilient in the face of this challenge and manage to get through this transition with a limited number of persistent symptoms and a new appreciation for life that was not always there before. In fact, for most women, symptoms gradually abate, energy levels recover, and new hair returns on the scalp. About a year after treatment ends, many women feel that they are back to most of their pre-illness physical activities. Specific groups for whom this is generally not true are those who are pushed into permanent menopause as a result of chemotherapy and those who require extensive and more disfiguring surgery (with or without reconstruction). The more intensive the therapy, however, the more likely a woman may be to suffer from fatigue, cognitive complaints, pain, and insomnia. This was dramatically seen in the women who underwent high-dose chemotherapy with bone marrow rescue during the early 1990s. Fortunately, such therapy is seldom given anymore as a result of its lack of efficacy, but current standard adjuvant chemotherapy is often much more intense than what was given a decade ago because supportive therapies (red and white cell growth factors) permit its use.

Today, for many women mammographic screening detects small breast tumors, which are treated with more limited breast surgery and removal of only a few lymph nodes from under the arm. The morbidity of this treatment is very modest, although follow-up breast radiation and endocrine therapy may cause problems for some women. Use of new genetic profiling tests in these instances can spare women toxic chemotherapy if it is unlikely to be helpful. However, how and why some women suffer persistent symptoms, and others do not, is an active area of research and investigation. This book calls important attention to the plight of these women, examining the struggles they face in having health care professionals, family members, and co-workers understand their experience and the impact of symptoms on their ability to function.

What can a woman with persistent and debilitating symptoms do under these circumstances? Must she suffer in silence, like many women described in this volume? The clear message from Abel and Subramanian is no. Bringing these ongoing problems out into the open gives them validity and is supportive to other women with symptoms after breast cancer who may read this book. The use of qualitative methods and the direct quotations from these breast cancer survivors enriches the book and provides an opportunity to identify with aspects of each woman's experience. Health care providers who read this book will develop a better appreciation for the need to attend to the ongoing symptoms of breast cancer survivors, as the consequences of neglect are many, as noted by the authors. For example, extended use of adjuvant endocrine therapy, especially the widely used aromatase inhibitors, is responsible for moderately severe ongoing symptoms in many breast cancer survivors. Failure to address these symptoms leads to diminished adherence to treatment, cheating women of the therapeutic benefit of highly effective therapy.

Increasingly, the posttreatment phase of cancer management is emphasizing survivorship care planning. In doing so, health care providers must focus on a palliative care approach that is symptom focused and values the subjective complaints of the breast cancer survivor. Acknowledging a woman's physical and emotional symptoms, even if they cannot all be abolished, will certainly go far in helping her to know that her health care team is concerned about her welfare. Supporting research that can further our understanding of the biological mechanisms underlying these persistent symptoms is the next step, which should facilitate more effective management strategies. Until then, as suggested by the authors, we should not ignore the dark side of breast cancer treatment. To recognize that these problems exist gives them legitimacy and supports those who experience the posttreatment sequelae of breast cancer.

Patricia A. Ganz, M.D.
Professor, UCLA Schools of Medicine and Public Health
Jonsson Comprehensive Cancer Center at UCLA

Introduction

WHEN EMILY ABEL finished six months of breast cancer surgery, chemotherapy, and radiation in 1993, she assumed her troubles were over. Doctors, friends, and family reassured her. She read scores of triumphalist breast cancer narratives; "Now I'm cured," they all pronounced by way of conclusion. And everywhere she looked, she saw ads for hospitals and pharmaceuticals displaying radiantly healthy cancer survivors, restored to their families and careers.

Emily soon realized, however, that breast cancer is a chronic condition. The disease can return at any time. Watchful waiting and second-guessing one's body never end. Every blood test and doctor's visit threatens to awaken what Alice Stewart Trillin dubbed "the dragon that sleeps inside anyone who has had cancer."[1] What was more unexpected was that lingering side effects of therapy also had made recovery elusive. When Emily complained about the overwhelming fatigue that persisted months and then years after finishing treatment, doctors explained that patients commonly experienced depression after cancer; perhaps she needed psychotherapy. Other breast cancer survivors, she was told, reported nothing like this.

But when Emily revealed her problems to other survivors, several confessed their own. They mentioned not only fatigue but also a panoply of other sensations they never before had experienced. She also spoke to adult children of survivors who recalled their mothers profoundly altered by breast cancer that had struck many years earlier. One mother had abandoned the tennis games that previously filled her mornings. Another had jettisoned a cherished career. If these women had "beaten" the cancer, then why did their lives seem so different?

Perhaps chemotherapy and radiation resembled other therapies that forestall death but often leave people with a raft of debilitating problems. The 1921 discovery of insulin, for example, dramatically extended the lives of diabetic patients, but they soon faced a new set of devastating symptoms.[2] The introduction of antiretrovirals in the 1990s converted an HIV diagnosis from a death sentence into a chronic disease for patients with access to the medication. Many breast cancer survivors, too, seemed to wrestle with an array of serious disabilities.

When she met Saskia Subramanian, a medical sociologist, Emily suggested a research topic to her: how women who have completed breast cancer chemotherapy and radiation cope with ongoing problems that doctors fail to take seriously. The more Saskia listened to Emily, the angrier she became. Given her training as a women's studies scholar, Saskia knew that male doctors sometimes labeled women's health complaints as psychosomatic and then dismissed them. During the same period, Saskia's mother was diagnosed with breast cancer, had surgery, and succumbed to the disease. Partly in her honor, Saskia began to read the proliferating sociological literature on patients' perspectives, which examines illness within the context of individual lives, as well as an emerging medical literature documenting posttreatment side effects.[3]

That research lent credibility to survivors' reports but left too many questions unanswered: What sense do women make of symptoms that persist long after the end of breast cancer treatment? What does it mean to live with these symptoms? How do cultural expectations of recovery shape women's experiences? How much do women blame themselves when they fail to return to their "normal" health? How can various symptoms affect personal relationships, work lives, leisure activities, and religious commitments? How do women react to doctors who fail to take the symptoms seriously? How do variations among women, by age, race, and socioeconomic status, affect their responses to the symptoms? The qualitative study we designed sought to address these issues.

With funding from the Susan G. Komen Foundation, we posted flyers at various sites, describing our study and inviting women to participate. Breast cancer survivors were eligible if they were at least one year beyond breast cancer treatment and believed they still were experiencing its physical, emotional, or cognitive effects. (We defined treatment as surgery, radiation, and chemotherapy; a few participants still were receiving Tamoxifen, a hormone therapy.) The final sample included thirty-six African American and thirty-eight white women, who were interviewed from one to three hours.[4]

We soon faced three thorny issues. First, how much credence should we give to symptoms that women reported but that physicians could not verify? The most common posttreatment symptoms are fatigue and cognitive impairment, both of which can be known only through patients' accounts.[5] Second, once we decided a woman's symptom was "real," how could we determine whether it was related to breast cancer treatment and therefore relevant to our research? Most studies are based on large populations, but it is notoriously difficult to make inferences from a group to an individual. Even if a study identified a particular condition as an aftereffect of cancer treatment within a population, how could we know whether it was caused by cancer in a particular case? And third, should we disregard symptoms that women reported but that have not been identified by researchers? Because our primary goal was to understand the lived experience of breast cancer survivors, we eventually decided to include in the study any conditions women both defined as problems and related, at least in part, to treatment. We are well aware, however, that doctors might interpret those conditions very differently.

Although we followed other researchers in asking about discrete symptoms, most women we interviewed experienced several simultaneously. Medical experts use the term "syndrome" to describe conditions with a cluster of diffuse symptoms, many of which may be only poorly understood. The more we listened to the women, the more we realized we might be hearing about a "post-breast-cancer syndrome." Survivors suffered from different symptoms. Individual symptoms interacted with others, intensifying the impact of each. And the accumulation of diverse symptoms often gave women the sense that their bodies and minds were falling apart.

We also discovered many parallels between the experiences of breast cancer survivors and people reporting symptoms of chronic fatigue syndrome, Gulf War syndrome, fibromyalgia (a chronic condition characterized by diffuse pain and severe fatigue), multiple chemical sensitivity, and irritable bowel syndrome. Like the sufferers of those invisible and often "contested" diseases, many women we interviewed went from doctor to doctor to find relief, employed various alternative and self-help measures, faced widespread skepticism about the existence of their troubles, and watched their social and work lives narrow.[6]

And yet, in many ways, the women in our study were distinctive. In the shadow of cancer, their experiences assumed special meaning. The doctors who refused to validate their symptoms were the same ones the women had depended on to provide life-saving treatments. The intimates who scoffed at survivors' ongoing complaints often had rendered essential support throughout months of chemotherapy and radiation. The work lives undermined by persistent symptoms already had been disrupted by the onset of cancer. And each symptom served as a constant reminder of the trauma of diagnosis, the ordeal of treatment, and the specter of recurrence.

To some extent, the stories we heard also closely resembled those told by other survivors. The current preoccupation with the disease has spawned a vast array of personal accounts, including illness narratives and reports of in-depth interviews, most of which focus on the period of diagnosis and treatment.[7] Because we wanted to understand how women's responses to posttreatment symptoms were intertwined with other life experiences, we asked many questions about diagnosis and treatment, and most chapters begin with a discussion of those events. Moreover, the trauma of diagnosis and treatment frequently remained so vivid that many women continued to focus on those events even after we tried to shift the conversation to the survivorship period; it was thus occasionally difficult to disentangle treatment from its aftermath. And, of course, some posttreatment symptoms do receive attention in existing accounts. Many women have written eloquently about the pain of lymphedema, the grief provoked by premature menopause and breast loss, and struggles with prostheses and reconstruction surgery. Not surprisingly, then, several themes that emerged from our interviews also figure prominently in other accounts. Various survivors explore the sense of profound alteration a breast cancer diagnosis provokes, attempts to remain in control of medical decisions, disappointment at friends and family members who fail to offer critical support, the need to withdraw from the workforce during treatment, and the spiritual awakenings that gradually enrich posttreatment lives.

Placing the broad range of posttreatment symptoms at the center of the discussion gives each of these themes a new dimension. The two most persistent problems, fatigue and cognitive impairment, were especially destructive to one's quality of life. Undermining cherished notions of self-esteem, both problems led to fear that continuity with the past had been irretrievably ruptured. Moreover, many symptoms we examine had received little medical acknowledgment when our interviewees began to experience them. Contending with problems about which doctors had little information impelled women not only to remain in charge of their medical care but also to question physician dominance over many aspects of their lives. Continuing fatigue and cognitive impairment impeded reentry into the workforce after the end of treatment. Some women who were able to work took jobs far beneath their qualifications. Finally, survivors struggling with a wide array of posttreatment symptoms had an especially intense need to reassess their priorities.

Readers may wonder why symptoms with such profound implications for survivors' lives received scant medical attention for many years. One reason may lie in the way drugs are tested. Pharmaceutical companies wishing to market new drugs must demonstrate proof that they are safe and effective before obtaining approval from the U.S. Food and Drug Administration. The clinical trials of chemotherapeutic agents tend to focus on survival rates rather than side effects. A recent study found that acute effects of chemotherapy, including hospitalizations and emergency-room visits, are far more common than expected.[8] It takes much longer for information about chronic effects to emerge. Moreover, two of the major long-term symptoms, fatigue and cognitive impairment, are especially difficult to measure and tend to rely on self-reporting.

Physicians' actions also may have been critical. Women undergoing the three types of cancer treatment (surgery, radiation, and chemotherapy) typically see surgeons, radiologists, and oncologists. It is possible those doctors disregarded early complaints from patients. Historically, physicians' quest for the rewards of professional status has rested on their claims to a monopoly of diagnostic competence. Throughout the nineteenth century, patients' accounts figured prominently in clinical assessments. Because disease was believed to arise from the particular interaction of individuals with their environment, universalistic knowledge of physiological processes was considered less important than personal knowledge of patients and the contexts of their lives. And, in the absence of virtually all diagnostic technologies, doctors had to listen to patients' reports about their bodies to make diagnoses.[9]

The rise of the health care system at the turn of the twentieth century dramatically reduced the status of those reports. That era enshrined the virtues of rationality, objectivity, neutrality, and universality. Knowledge accorded the honorific title "scientific" received special veneration. An accumulation of breakthroughs enabled physicians to transform themselves into a powerful and privileged profession. The isolation of the pathogens causing major infectious diseases rendered irrelevant personal information about specific individuals. Simultaneously, the development of new diagnostic tools including x-ray machines, microscopes, and bacteriological tests permitted physicians to bypass patients' accounts entirely.[10] Some observers argue that the inability of doctors to discern pain through "objective" tests continues to impede efforts to study it.[11] Perhaps doctors ignored survivors' reports about persistent fatigue and cognitive impairment for a similar reason.

Other factors also may influence physician behavior today. Insurance companies place increasing pressure on doctors to see as many patients as possible within the shortest period of time, and few medical schools provide adequate training in communication with patients.[12] Moreover, doctors traditionally have been especially quick to dismiss women's complaints as psychosomatic. After surveying a wide array of studies, a medical sociologist concluded that women are "particularly vulnerable" to psychosomatic diagnoses "because women visit doctors more than men, because women reportedly have more 'functional' complaints (complaints about symptoms for which a doctor finds no organic explanation), because more women have histories of being diagnosed with depression, and because medicine knows less about women's bodies."[13]

The public, too, may have been disinclined to focus on the negative, long-term effects of chemotherapy and radiation. Americans have long considered themselves a uniquely blessed people, immune to the normal vicissitudes of life. Alexis de Tocqueville famously described the country as "a course almost without limits, a field without horizon," a place where "the human spirit rushes forward . . . in every direction."[14] And, for more than a century, medicine has served as the epitome of the country's promise, offering rejuvenation and renewal to all. Dazzled by widely heralded discoveries, we minimize the failures of medical wizardry and the complicated realities of patients' lives.[15]

The history of breast cancer during the past hundred years offers a case in point. Despite the dramatic changes that have occurred in the medical treatment of the disease, a single theme dominates that history: the cultural denial of vulnerability and contingency has severely restricted the topics that can be discussed. At the turn of the twentieth century, breast cancer was associated with some of the most terrible, lingering deaths and thus remained highly invisible. Patients often failed to disclose their diagnoses, even to intimates, and doctors routinely listed other causes on death certificates.[16]

After its creation in 1913, the American Society for the Control of Cancer (later the American Cancer Society) engendered a new openness about the disease without unsettling the traditional evasion of disability and death. Substituting positive stereotypes for negative ones, the organization encouraged women to participate in early detection. By World War II, a massive health-education campaign had developed in the United States, promising that breast cancer would neither kill nor maim any woman who remained vigilant, regularly examined her breasts, and reported all suspicious signs to her doctor. The devastating consequences of the reigning treatment were almost completely ignored. Since the turn of the twentieth century, most doctors had followed Johns Hopkins University surgeon William Stewart Halsted, who pioneered radical mastectomies for breast cancer.[17] That operation caused serious chest deformities, including hollow areas under the collarbones and armpits, and, in some cases, lymphedema (arm or hand swelling), pain, and mobility problems.[18]

"For a disease that engendered secrecy in the first place," one historian writes, "the details and consequences of radical surgery remained the most hidden aspect of breast cancer."[19] The many films, posters, books, and magazine articles distributed by the American Cancer Society neither described nor depicted women with surgical scars. One doctor asserted that radical surgery left "no important disability or deformity." Another advised women to "put an old stocking in their bra" and forget about the disease.[20]

Some critics did challenge the dominant discourse. A growing chorus of doctors argued that breast cancer was a systemic rather than a local disease, that early detection could not save the lives of women with aggressive tumors, and that radical mastectomies were no more effective than less extensive procedures.[21] A rare 1937 novel described the Halsted mastectomy as "mutilating." And a few survivors publicly revealed the physical and emotional problems they suffered.[22]

But those discussions quickly led to a new campaign to deny the aftereffects of breast cancer. Scientific advances during World War II enabled manufacturers to create breast prostheses for cancer survivors. A major advocate of their use was the founder of Reach to Recovery, Terese Lasser. In a magazine article entitled "I Had Breast Cancer," Lasser declared, "A deplorable curtain of silence hangs about this subject and it is time we lift it."[23] Lasser attempted to breach that silence by organizing a cadre of survivors to visit other women immediately after surgery. Simultaneously, however, she intensified the secrecy surrounding mastectomies. Reach to Recovery volunteers preached that the prostheses could not only conceal breast loss but also facilitate healing.[24]

Similar messages of hope and optimism infused the breast cancer narratives that began to appear in the 1970s. Publicity surrounding the diagnoses of Betty Ford, the wife of President Gerald Ford, and Happy Rockefeller, the wife of Vice President Nelson Rockefeller, encouraged other survivors to chronicle their experiences. Marvella Bayh, the wife of Senator Birch Bayh of Indiana, recalled a visit from a Reach to Recovery volunteer: "I just stared at this woman who looked like a model, and I thought to myself: If she can do it, I can too!"[25] Helga Sandburg Crile, the daughter of poet Carl Sandburg and the wife of an iconoclastic breast cancer surgeon, wrote that she thanked her "lucky stars that all had gone well" in her "adventure."[26] Even Betty Rollin, whose popular *First, You Cry* ridiculed the "Pollyanna" tone of other illness narratives, later emphasized her return to normality, comparing herself to a car with a "dent" in its "fender."[27]

The seventies also witnessed the development of a new cosmetic fix. Poet Audre Lorde famously denounced breast reconstruction as an "atrocity" because it hid the effects of a terrible disease.[28] Nevertheless, the popularity of the procedure grew rapidly; doctors performed twenty thousand reconstructions in 1981 alone.[29] Grateful patients tended to be even more emphatic than prosthesis wearers that they had success-fully surmounted the disease. The author of *I Am Whole Again*, for ex-ample, asserted, "The whole cancer experience was behind me, shelved, at last, pushed out of daily consciousness."[30]

Although a combination of accumulating scientific evidence, patient dissatisfaction, and women's health activism convinced the majority of surgeons to abandon the Halsted mastectomy by the end of the seven-ties, posttreatment effects did not disappear. Most patients avoided the terrible disfigurement of radical surgery, but pain, numbness, scar tis-sue, and lymphedema continued to plague a significant proportion. The growing use of breast reconstruction inflicted additional difficulties. And the rise of radiation therapy and chemotherapy created a whole new set of problems. First introduced at the turn of the twentieth century, radia-tion became far more prominent as lumpectomies (breast-conserving surgery) increasingly replaced mastectomies in the 1980s and 1990s. Chemotherapy emerged from the World War II discovery that nitro-gen mustard gas retarded the growth of cells.[31] By the late 1970s, doc-tors were employing various chemotherapeutic agents not only to treat women whose disease had spread but also to prevent that development in high-risk women.[32] During the 1990s, some women with advanced cancer began to receive extremely aggressive regimes, including unusu-ally high doses of chemotherapy followed by bone marrow transplanta-tion. (That procedure was abandoned, however, after large randomized trials reported it had no benefits.)[33] Although doctors initially remained silent about the long-term consequences of both radiation and chemo-therapy, patients soon began to complain about a host of difficulties. And, of course, regardless of the type of therapy employed, survivors continued to worry that the disease would return. Despite the steady drop in the breast cancer mortality rate since 1995, women are well aware that the disease still claims thousands of lives each year.[34]

The enormous flowering of breast cancer activism since the 1990s has given the disease greater visibility than ever before. Far from concealing their diagnoses, survivors proclaim their new identities.

The tone is relentlessly upbeat. Now a woman can not only survive breast cancer but also emerge greatly improved. After singer Melissa Etheridge finished breast cancer treatment in 2005, ABC News described her as "stronger, better, and more passionate about life than ever before."[35] Dozens of teams, clubs, and organizations promote and publicize survivors' participation in physically challenging endeavors, including dragon-boat competitions, lengthy bike rides, walks, races, and mountain climbs.

One of the most trenchant critics of the optimism of the current breast cancer movement is Barbara Ehrenreich, whose widely circulated essay "Welcome to Cancerland" argues that the flip side of the glorification of survivorship is the denigration of the dead and seriously ill. "Did we who live 'fight' harder than those who've died?" she asks. "Can we claim to be 'braver,' better people than the dead?"[36] Even Ehrenreich, however, ignores another major group of women missing from the celebratory breast cancer culture—those whose treatment side effects fail to abate. Ehrenreich notes only the difficulties chemotherapy and radiation temporarily inflict and defines "chemobrain" as "short term" mental deterioration."[37]

This book tells the stories of survivors who must learn to live with, find remedies for, and assign meaning to a broad array of problems that persist long after therapy ends. Although the book draws on all seventy-four of the interviews we conducted, eleven women dominate the account. The information in the following profiles was current at the time of the interviews.[38]

Marge Barlow

A forty-nine-year-old white woman with short, curly hair, Marge Barlow explained why she rarely mentions her illness experience to family members: "My mother's whole family died of cancer by the time they were in their midsixties. And she's had melanomas and multiple surgeries, and right now my father is in his third cancer, and he's probably going to die from this one." Nevertheless, the family has "a lot of resistance to taking any point of view other than 'keep a positive attitude and you can beat this,' even though there is absolutely nothing in our experience to support that attitude."

Marge's own disease struck when she was in the middle of a sociology Ph.D. program. After practicing law in Chicago for fifteen years, she moved across the country to pursue a career she hoped to find more meaningful. Although fellowships and savings provided a decent living, she was impatient to finish school, find a job, and regain the rewards of professional status. But when posttreatment cognitive impairment hindered her ability to write her dissertation, she began to reassess her commitment to academia.

Annie Briggs

A deep sense of anger and sadness pervaded our interview with Annie Briggs, a forty-four-year-old African American woman. Growing up gay, she often felt "ostracized" by her mother and siblings. "They were not the supporting family that I would have asked for if I could go out and pick." Her mother's comments especially wounded: "Telling me to just lean on the Lord for everything. You cannot lean on the Lord. He sees billions of people. He's got billions of people He's trying to carry through." Annie felt as if her mother was "coming at" her "like an axe."

An ex-Marine, Annie worked as an inspector at a petroleum plant until persistent symptoms from breast cancer treatment forced her to quit; now she has difficulty making ends meet. Although our interview took place on the fourth anniversary of her diagnosis, it was not a happy occasion. Her doctor had just told her that the breast cancer had returned in her breast and that she faced additional surgery and chemotherapy.

Marsha Dixler

Marsha Dixler is determined to forget the messages she learned as a child. A divorced, fifty-year-old African American woman, she works as a trust administrator in a bank. "I'm from Arkansas," she said, "and Arkansas was black and white. The doctors were white and the patients were black. When the doctor told you something, it was 'OK.' Whatever it is, 'OK.' With me coming from there, I still have that mentality. Whatever they would say, 'OK.'" Since receiving a mastectomy, chemotherapy, and radiation in 1996, Marsha has experienced cognitive dysfunction and serious back pain. A major fear is that she could "fall through the cracks" at the large cancer center where she receives follow-up care:

> Paperwork isn't faxed; paperwork isn't received. So therefore I have to do a lot of it; I have to stay on top of it. On many occasions I've called and said that I wasn't feeling good or something was going on, but I did not get a call back. I got to the point where I did everything. If you want something faxed, I'll fax you. [The doctor would] get a little intimidated when I'd type up a whole letter. But see, I'm working too. I can't sit on the phone and hold a half day to get in touch with you. That's taking time away from my job. That's not fair to my company and my employer that I'm there and talking to you all the time, trying to get in touch with you over and over again.

Pat Garland

Pat Garland is an African American woman who looks much younger than her fifty-five years. Her dark hair pulled back from her face falls just past her shoulders. Speaking slowly and with great deliberation, she told us that when she underwent a mastectomy and chemotherapy, she joined a support group for white women as well as one for blacks. One reason was her conviction that white women had unique access to the most up-to-date information. In addition, she feared African American women too frequently view breast cancer as simply one more trouble they must learn to bear. "They say, 'This is another trauma. Do I need to ask the doctor any questions? No. Do I need to understand the verbiage that he's using? No.' And that's very, very dangerous." White women, in her view, are "the fighting women of breast cancer."

But when treatment left Pat with several debilitating symptoms, she discovered that assertiveness is not enough. Despite her best efforts, she could not obtain adequate diagnoses or remedies. Although her severe joint pain prevents her from working, she is unable to claim the disability benefits to which she is entitled.

Ida Jaffe

A fifty-eight-year-old African American woman, Ida Jaffe is a magnetically warm woman who has a direct, no-nonsense manner. She explained why she waited a year between finding a breast lump and bringing it to medical attention: "I did not know that black women got cancer. I don't remember seeing a black woman on a poster or hearing black women say they have cancer. Mostly all of the advertisements you see are white women. Therefore, we're kind of left out of the loop." Determined to learn as much as possible about the disease, she, too, joined both white and African American support groups.

By the time she finally saw an oncologist, Ida's cancer had spread, and she received an extremely aggressive therapy, including a mastectomy, high-dose chemotherapy, and bone marrow transplantation. Although she returned to her administrative job at the post office soon after treatment ended, she finally realized that memory loss prevented her from functioning at her previous level and decided to quit.

Rose Jensen

A fifty-two-year-old white woman with light hair and blue eyes, Rose Jensen had a mastectomy and chemotherapy in 1995. Although her diagnosis strained her already shaky marriage, she and her husband decided to remain together: "I wanted to know what my statistical probability of survival was based on the lymph node involvement and the size of the tumor, and when you did the math, it really wasn't very optimistic. I really think my ex-husband thought I was going to die. And so we stayed in a very toxic marriage because I didn't want to expose the children, who were four and eight, to a difficult divorce and then die on them." Five years later, however, the marriage finally dissolved:

> My oncologist mentioned to me that I had hit my five-year milestone, which at that point I thought meant something. I came home and just sort of related over dinner that it had been five years. And my mother was there, and she got up and she was excited and she was hugging me, and the girls were, "Hooray, hooray." And

my husband's response was so diametrically opposed; it was like, "You've hit your milestone?" And he just sort of looked at me and said, "Well, I guess you're not going to die, huh?" And I said, "No, at least not now." And within months he had found someone else.

Rose's divorce accentuates the economic problems she has faced since persistent cognitive impairment forced her to abandon her high-paying engineering career.

Tessa McKnight

Tessa McKnight, a tall, slim, forty-one-year-old white woman, said that the flower shop she opened six years before her diagnosis provided some of her deepest joy throughout the many months of surgery, chemotherapy, and radiation. Beauty surrounded her, and she viewed herself "creating art" whenever she arranged flowers. But her clientele dwindled when self-care took precedence over work, and by the end of treatment, a huge debt had accumulated. Now she has to struggle to shed a deep sense of shame about her financial difficulties: "It is hard for me to not identify that with myself. I have to go, 'I'm not this debt. I have this debt, but I'm not a bad person because I have it.'"

Posttreatment symptoms created additional identity issues. She is unable to lose the forty pounds she gained during treatment, has little energy, has experienced premature menopause, and suffers from depression and arthritis. "You don't end up the same person that you started," she concludes.

Greta Shaw

Greta Shaw is a forty-eight-year-old white woman with reddish hair who lives in the San Fernando Valley. Contemplating her parents' experiences, she wonders why she cannot so easily put her cancer behind her. Since lung cancer surgery several years ago, her father has enjoyed good health. Her mother has never complained about the aftereffects of the mastectomy she received in her sixties, and her cancer has not returned.

But Greta had chemotherapy and radiation as well as breast surgery, and she experiences an array of symptoms. Her major one is a mouth sore, which is virtually invisible but blunts the taste of food and inflicts intense, burning pain. More than any other woman in our study, Greta faces questions about the legitimacy of her suffering. Whereas other survivors eventually receive at least some confirmation that their symptoms are real, Greta's mouth problem remains unrecognized.

Leanne Thomas

Leanne Thomas is no stranger to trouble. A fifty-five-year-old African American woman, she saw her mother and three aunts die of breast cancer before she received her own diagnosis in 2001. A car accident ten years earlier left her with such severe back problems that she was forced to relinquish her job as a bank teller; since then, she has lived on less than ten thousand dollars a year. Now she has to deal not only with anxiety about a recurrence but also with a panoply of posttreatment symptoms, including hot flashes, dental and vision problems, insomnia, memory loss, fatigue, and depression.

When we interviewed her in her small, dark apartment, however, she focused less on those calamities than on a friend's death. "Recently I've been dreaming about my girlfriend," she told us.

> She's deceased, and I've dreamed about her the past couple of nights. She was on dialysis. Her kidneys failed her, and she was a diabetic. We were very close friends, grew up in school together. I'm seeing her now. We're going out eating and talking and everything. I went to dialysis with her and made sure she was being taken care of and they knew me. "Here comes this lady with this notebook, and she's writing down everything, and she's going to report it." I made sure that she got everything that she needed. When she was in the hospital, I made sure that everything was taken care of. She was at Martin Luther King Hospital, and she asked me, "Don't let me die in here." And she smiled, and I knew she was serious. They did take her home, and she did die at home.

Does Leanne see herself in her friend, another woman with a life-threatening illness? Do the dreams sharpen Leanne's sense of loneliness? Since her friend's death, Leanne has lacked a dependable source of support as she contends with her own serious health problems.

Jean Trawick

A petite, intense, white, sixty-three-year-old divorced woman, Jean Trawick remembers herself as "a very spoiled child." Her father was a doctor, "so it was like, 'Hey, Joe, my daughter's coming over. Take care of her.' And I'd waltz in and get good services, and they would care about me." But Jean's father died shortly before her first cancer diagnosis, in 1984, when she had a lumpectomy and radiation. "Suddenly I didn't have those contacts, and I assumed, wrongly so, that doctors would take care of me. They didn't. . . . It's not OK to have doctors cut you open and violate you, even in the name of saving your life. That doesn't mean I can't have gratitude for them, but it's a brutal way to be taken care of, and then you add on the rudeness and insensitivity of lots of people in lots of different ways. It is not OK."

Her saga began a few days after her lumpectomy, when she returned to her surgeon's office for a follow-up visit. "He said, 'Let me take a look at your arm.' And he took it, and he yanked it, and when he yanked it, it was extremely painful. I remember that to this day, and when I called him later and said, 'I can't move my arm now,' he said, 'Nothing to do with the surgery, nothing to do with the surgery.'" She was determined to find a more congenial physician: "I made contact with a surgeon out in the Valley who I thought was well recommended and trustworthy. I saw him every six months for a checkup. I had a real good rapport, I thought." But eight years after her lumpectomy, her cancer returned, and their relationship dissolved. When she announced her intention to get a second opinion, he erupted in anger. Although she had no complaints about the surgeon who performed both her mastectomy and the reconstruction, her various posttreatment symptoms put her "on a road to look for other things." Her primary-care provider now is a nurse practitioner "who deals with chronic illness and who knows both Western and alternative medicines."

Nina Worth

Nina Worth was all too familiar with cancer when she received her diagnosis in 2001. A thirty-seven-year-old white woman with a ready smile, she works at a major university cancer center. Although her job is in fund-raising rather than direct patient care, she encounters very sick and dying patients whenever she leaves her office. Ten years before she learned she had breast cancer, she had been treated for Hodgkin's disease. That experience convinced her she would have to resign herself to a solitary life. While undergoing chemotherapy for breast cancer, however, she met an old friend and discovered he was able to share the burden of her pain. After treatment ended, they married:

> For as long as I can remember, I really never thought I would find someone who would be able to go through the process of watching me deal with cancer and be a part of that and be a support in that. And frankly the only way that could be proved to me was to actually have someone do that. And that's what my husband did, and I could see him do that. He didn't run, and he held me. So, you know, as much as I despise this disease, in fact it took that to bring us together in a strange and bizarre way. And it took that for me to be able to trust him, that in fact he really could work through this with me.

Now they must face new challenges together. She experiences memory loss, joint pain, and vaginal dryness, which makes sexual intercourse difficult. And the chemotherapy drugs pushed her into premature menopause. Unless her menses return, she will be unable to bear the child they both desperately desire.

In what follows we attempt to understand the meaning of posttreatment symptoms by placing them within the context of these individual women's lives.

1

"Standing on New Ground"

ALTHOUGH MEDICAL RESEARCHERS have begun to investigate a number of posttreatment symptoms, we wanted to know how survivors themselves understood their various complaints. Greta Shaw began by discussing a problem that is virtually absent from the existing literature:

One of the roughest things is that a month after I finished radiation I woke up with a salty taste in my mouth. The salty taste in my mouth has basically stayed and never left. Certain days are worse than others, and along with the saltiness as time went on I have this area on the side of my tongue that feels like it's a sore, and it never goes away. My whole entire mouth area has given me a lot of problems. I even have a huge thing on the side of my face that's kind of always there inside, you know, where the gum is. That always bothers me, and this past week, oddly enough, there was a huge, ulcerated kind of canker sore on that area as well. It comes and goes and gets worse at different times. But it really is very, very painful. And I can't even tell you how many doctors I have been to for this, numerous doctors. . . . I've cried in doctors' offices over this. And because you don't see all that much, they don't think that there's a lot of pain. You can kind of see a little bit, but nothing like, "Wow, it's there." And sometimes even my mouth will like quiver with all of the trauma of this area. It will have little spasms. It's altered my taste buds; things don't taste like they did. I don't crave like everybody else does. I just go, "Oh, that sounds OK." Nothing sounds that great. Believe it or not, it's really been one of the worst and hardest things to live with. Sometimes I feel like I just have to put something in my mouth to just try to curb it, because it gets so intense. It's painful, it burns, and it's salty, and it's just bizarre.

Like many women, Greta faces several problems simultaneously. When we asked if she had any other symptoms, she responded,

Yeah! That's the one that's the weirdest, the most peculiar. But of course I have. I went into chemo-induced menopause. That has been, of course, very tough. It's what they call crash menopause, and the symptoms just come on overnight. And when it happens you don't even know if it's the chemo or what's going on. So in hindsight, when I look back, a lot of the stuff I have been feeling may have been due to the menopause, with all the hot flashes and sweats and that whole thing.

I've had all the symptoms of menopause, horrible, horrible, horrible vaginal dryness, which I know is a huge thing. It's just ridiculous. Actually I'm unable to have sexual intercourse right now. It's too painful. And I would love to know if that's really common because my gynecologist is saying, "Yes, it's common, it's common," but she kind of doesn't understand why it isn't maybe a little bit better than it is. Like when I have my pap [smears] and stuff, it's really painful now.

I'm always afraid to even try anything just because it's so painful. It's ridiculous. And that's caused a lot of problems as far as, of course, being married. I mean it has caused a lot of friction. And, of course, there's no sexual desire or anything like that; that's just a given. Everything's gone. I don't ever think about it; the libido is just out the door.

And then the brain, the brain's bad, embarrassingly bad. People that know me, I'm fine with. They all understand because they just have kind of gotten used to it. Though I think some of them are kind of afraid because it is really bad; certain days are better than others. Like I was thinking you were coming and I'm going, "Hmmm, I wonder if I'm going to have a really foggy day or a pretty clear day." And you know, I'm pretty good today. You can even see it in my eyes when it's bad. It's just kind of scary because I just get really like fatigued—how do I put it?—brain exhausted. It's embarrassing; it really is. I have really wondered how much longer I would be able to work if this got really bad. I've had times where at work I've thought "OK"—and conversations with my husband—"how am I going to do this? How am I going to continue to work?" And I need to work; it's not like I can afford not to work. I don't think I could even go to another job and try to learn something. I can't imagine what that would be like. I'd be so scared. And I've thought about it just because I feel like, you know, sometimes at work I would feel like they were saying something about me maybe behind my back about it. That's really hard because I used to be pretty sharp—I mean, not like over and above. I just feel like I used to be a lot sharper; I could think straight. I think sometimes people don't quite understand, and they just think that maybe you're kind of dumb just because I left my job of ten years and I went there. So the people that I worked with before then knew who I was. These people really don't know who I was before. I've even said, you know, "I used to be a lot sharper."

And there's another thing it's complicated to note. I'm approaching forty-nine years old. Would menopause have been just like this for a regular person? Or is it because of the chemo? I can't figure any of it out.

Of course, when you're on the chemo and everything, everything is really foggy, and then afterwards for the first year I think a lot of it was kind of a combination of that and being really physically drained. I had a lot of chemo. I had like eleven rounds. So I had a lot of stuff. And so I'd say that for the following year it was just kind of such a combo. But I almost think that my brain has gotten even worse lately in the past year. I know that the moment-to-moment remember-what-I'm-doing kind of thing is bad. And I know people say this all the time, "Well, I go from one room, and I can't remember what I'm doing in the other room." But for some reason it feels different. And I don't know how to explain it. Maybe I'm wrong, but I think it feels different than if it were to happen to you or my husband or whatever. Maybe anybody would feel this way. How do you know? You don't know.

The genesis of aches and pains also causes confusion:

> I am approaching fifty. People say things start getting kind of . . . , you know. I think I have definitely more joint pain than I used to have, and it did start back then, and it hasn't gone away. But just in general, my stiffness in joints and my knees, even my hips, my feet. But, you know, I work on my feet, so how the heck do I know? They're just kind of swollen, and they feel like there's kind of pins and needles in them a lot. It could be circulation.

Greta reported other symptoms in response to our questions. By the end of the interview, she had added lymphedema, anxiety, depression, dental problems, and scar tissue to her list.

"Still Waiting to Find Me Again"

All through the long, dark months of breast cancer treatment, patients look forward to the moment it will end and ordinary life resume. Many, however, still feel profoundly altered a year or more afterward. We repeatedly heard comments such as the following:

> That's the story they don't tell, that you don't go back to the life you had.

> All the treatment is over, it just seems like I'm still not back to me. I'm still waiting to find me again.

> I kind of came out maybe not a different person, but definitely standing on new ground.

> I'm happy to have a life, but it's not the same quality of life that I had before.

> A part of me has been buried along with my right breast.

Some survivors spoke in terms of aging:

I feel ten years older.

I feel like an old lady; I got old very fast.

Now I have to behave like a real elderly person.

I've aged tremendously.

The sense of radical change derived partly from the trauma of diagnosis and treatment. A philosopher defines a traumatic event as "one in which a person feels utterly helpless in the face of a force that is perceived to be life-threatening. The immediate psychological responses to such trauma include terror, loss of control, and intense fear of annihilation."[1] An element of surprise can increase the likelihood of long-term harm.[2] After receiving treatment for Hodgkin's disease, Nina Worth had been "kind of waiting for this [cancer] experience to happen": "It was always there in the back of my mind. And it was not a surprise to me when Dr. P. called me and told me what they had found." The great majority of women, however, insisted breast cancer had appeared without warning. Several had expected good health habits to confer immunity. "I think it's recommended after forty that you start getting mammograms," one said. "I haven't missed a year since I turned forty, and I think that's why I was so shocked when this happened. I just could not believe it. I've been getting a mammogram every year; how come all of a sudden this came up?" Another woman described herself as "a runner and a Trader Joe addict": "I mean, I can't live without food, but I'm not into grease or alcohol. I watched my diet and worked out and slept and did all the normal things that people are supposed to do to stay within good health." Her youth, too, was supposed to offer protection: "I thought old people get cancer. I mean no disrespect to elders, but I'm thinking I have more miles to go." Although the incidence of many serious diseases (including breast cancer) increases sharply with age, a seventy-one-year-old woman stated, "My father lived to ninety in a very active life, and it didn't dawn on me that things could change. It was a rude awakening. . . . I just went for my routine mammogram, and the next thing I know, before the end of that evening, it was pretty evident that I had cancer. Not a clue, not a symptom, not a pain. So it was really a bolt out of the blue."

Injury to the body also can intensify the toxic effects of trauma.[3] Although most women felt completely well at the time of diagnosis, treatment inflicted physical damage. Several survivors underlined their sense of violation by using Dr. Susan Love's famous description of surgery, chemotherapy, and radiation as "slash, poison, and burn."[4] Others raged against euphemisms that disguised treatment horrors. "I just burst out sobbing when I heard that I had to have chemotherapy," one woman recalled, "and I said, 'But it's so toxic, it's so poisonous.' The doctor's like, 'Well, we don't like to use the word "poisonous."' But wait a minute. If it's toxic, it's poisonous." Pat Garland said, "If I had lost an arm or whatever, people would be giving me therapy and they would understand and there would be empathy. But there was none of that, and they amputated my breast. They don't call it 'amputation'; they call it 'mastectomy.' I wonder why they changed the name? Is it because it's a woman?"

One sign of trauma is a desire to discuss the traumatic event over and over.[5] Because our study focused on the period after surgery, chemotherapy, and radiation, we asked very few specific questions about those events. Most women, however, took advantage of the interviews as another opportunity to retell their treatment stories. A survivor vividly remembered going home after a mastectomy:

> I had a drain, and I had to keep measuring that and emptying that, and mine got clogged a couple of times, so I had to go to the emergency room for that. . . . I remember the first Sunday after I got through the surgery, I went to church. I wear big clothes anyway, so I had the big clothes with the drain hanging out. And the bandages. It was kind of scary to get into the shower because I didn't know what that was gonna do. So it was the unknown, the unknown.

Several women focused on chemotherapy. One remarked,

> I had never gone through anything like that before. The way it makes you feel, you can't sleep, you can't stand up, you can't eat. You just feel strange. I guess it's all the drugs and everything. After

you take the treatment I've noticed that I could be up for a couple of days, but then after that I would be down for about four or five days. Then I notice that after I got more and more into the treatment what would happen is I wouldn't be up as long. I would go down faster, and I'd stay longer down. What could I do? I couldn't do anything but stay in bed, and I'd have the food right there by my bedside. And then my hair loss—oh gosh. When that came out, I said, "Didn't you say that it might not come out? But it did come out." And I'm being very positive: "I'm not going to lose my hair. It's still in here." And I'd just comb it, and all the stuff came out. I didn't like losing all of your hair everywhere. No eyebrows—you look like a bald-headed doll with no eyebrows, no nothing. And I couldn't stand to look at myself in the mirror with no hair, with a bald head.

Marsha Dixler described her high-dose chemotherapy treatment as "the worst experience of my life. A couple of times I tried to find the back door out of the doctor's office and figured out how I can go from this third floor, go out the window, because I didn't want that chemo again. It was that horrible."

For Tessa McKnight, radiation was "even harder than the chemo." "It was just so lonely. People would come to chemo with me. Radiation is something you have to go to by yourself every day, and you're alone in the room. The people can't even be there with you. And you're just [with] all these machines. There's no pain or anything, except your breast gets fried. That was hard."

And breast cancer was never over. Although all the women in our study were considered cancer-free at the time of the interviews, twelve had had recurrences. One explained why she kept her wedding simple: "I thought, 'What if something would have happened in between a long year of planning and trying on dresses and wedding chapels and cakes and planning and planning and planning?' I don't think I could have done it, to be that confident that I'm going to live, oh wow, another year." Having experienced two different types of cancer, Nina Worth remarked, "My husband thinks much more long-term than I do. Even though we're planning for retirement and have life insurance and all that kind of stuff, the vision of that for me is just so removed."

Even women who had had only one cancer diagnosis claimed that unfinished life tasks assumed new urgency. Rose Jensen refused to call herself a "survivor" until she had successfully brought up her children, still in elementary school. A second woman worried about her grandson: "He needs so much. He needs extra care because my daughter is not always tuned in to what she needs to do with him. And I worry who's gonna taken care of him if something happens to me."

Periodic examinations served as reminders not only of the original trauma but also of the possibility that the cancer could return at any time. "It's been ten years since I had the mastectomy," a woman told us, "and even going for checkups has that level of tension and anxiety about it. About two weeks ago, I went to UCLA and had a mammogram ultrasound. And it was normal, it was fine. So I go and I have an exam with the surgeon, and she goes, 'What's this lump? What's this lump?' And I just panicked again." Her terror persisted long after she learned scar tissue had caused the thickness. Another survivor commented,

> A lot of people think cancer happens to somebody else, like "Oh, I'm not going to get cancer." But now that I've had the diagnosis, it's changed my life in that it's always this cloud above me, like, "Is it going to come back? How is this test going to go? How's the result of this test going to be?" There's always a lot of anxiety as I'm waiting for test results because suppose in a mammogram they see another lump and then they're going to have to check again. Maybe kind of holding your breath. And people say, "Well anybody can get cancer; people get diagnosed all the time." That doesn't help me. I'm already in the cancer club. I'm a member for life.

The deaths of other breast cancer survivors sharpened fears. "I've seen too many people who'd die, and they didn't make it," a woman said. "And they were talking like I am today and gone tomorrow. I hate to say this, but it's the constant fear like, 'Oh, what's that pain?' Like even if I'm walking out and I got to catch my breath, I'm like, 'Why'd it do that, Lord?' I'm constantly listening to my body more than I ever did."

Symptoms

Above all, enduring health problems encouraged survivors to view their lives as profoundly altered. Table 1.1 indicates the prevalence of the major complaints reported to us. (Because many women reported multiple symptoms, the percentages add up to more than 100).

TABLE 1.1
NUMBER AND PERCENTAGE OF WOMEN
REPORTING SYMPTOMS

Symptom	Number	Percentage
Arthritis in hands	28	38%
Arthritis in knees/other joints	35	47%
Headaches/migraines	22	30%
Soreness in breast area	48	65%
Problems moving arms	29	39%
Soreness or numbness under arm	46	62%
Lack of sleep/insomnia	47	64%
Fatigue	52	70%
Inability to concentrate	34	46%
Forgetfulness/memory loss	57	70%
Depression	38	51%
Anxiety	31	42%
Early onset menopause	31	42%
Painful intercourse	19	26%
Loss of sex drive	35	47%
Lymphedema	24	32%
Dental or mouth problems	13	18%
Other	64	86%

Because we interviewed only women who identified themselves as experiencing postcancer symptoms, the rates in table 1.1 undoubtedly are much higher than would be expected among a random sample of breast cancer survivors.[6] Nevertheless, it is clear that at least some survivors experience a large burden of ill health.

Some symptoms were relatively straightforward. For example, doctors have long known that the drug Adriamycin, often administered to women with the later stages of the disease, leads to congestive heart problems in a small proportion of patients and that various chemother-apeutic agents can cause premature menopause in women over forty.[7] (Because menopausal changes occur abruptly rather than gradually over several years, they tend to be especially intense, hence the term "crash menopause.") The consequences of surgery also are well under-stood. The most serious is lymphedema, an accumulation of lymph fluid, which can cause infection and lymphangiosarcoma, a rare form of cancer; other complications include disfigurement, restricted move-ment, and physical discomfort. "I have pain, pain," one woman told us. "I'm talking on the telephone, and I have to watch myself and switch because the arm starts to hurt. Or it's hurting when I'm driving. And then my wrist started aching a couple of weeks ago, so I thought, 'Oh, how much more pain is there going to be?'" Although the incidence of lymphedema dropped sharply after the introduction of sentinel node biopsy in the late 1990s, the majority of women in this study received the older procedure.

The origin of many other posttreatment complaints, however, is unclear. Recent studies report that in addition to congestive heart fail-ure, premature menopause, and lymphedema, the late effects of breast cancer can include psychosocial distress, arthritis, fatigue, and cogni-tive impairment. But some women we interviewed blamed the disease and its treatment for a range of other problems as well. Moreover, breast cancer is not always the primary cause even of problems that are in-cluded in the medical literature. As a report published jointly by the In-stitute of Medicine and the National Research Council of the National Academies points out, "It is sometimes difficult to distinguish among cancer-related changes, age-related changes, and those caused by co-morbid conditions."[8] Co-morbid conditions are other health problems the survivors experience distinct from cancer or the aging process.

Several women in our study shared that confusion. Greta noted that "a lot of the stuff" she experienced might have been "due to the menopause." Poor circulation as well as her approaching age fifty might explain her aches and pains. When we asked a woman in her seventies whether she attributed her memory difficulties to cancer treatment, she responded, "At first I did, but then when I'm with a peer, they say, 'Well, I'm forgetful.' So I don't know. I really don't know." Asked about any cognitive symptoms, another woman responded, "I have all that, but I think it's age. I mean, it's very hard to distinguish. You see I got cancer when I was fifty-seven or fifty-eight, and that's when all these things start happening anyway, so it's hard for me to know if those things are related to it or if it's just a natural process." Some midlife women wondered if chemotherapy had precipitated the menopause or if that change would have occurred then anyway.

There were other questions as well. Was a knee problem the result of cancer treatment, weight gain, or the reactivation of a childhood injury? Did depression contribute to the fatigue? Could a failure to exercise the brain after retirement have helped to cause the cognitive decline? Was a woman more anxious because she had received a terrifying diagnosis and undergone a harrowing treatment, because her husband had left her, or because she was "evolving into a more anxious, nervous type"? Greta thus probably spoke for many survivors when she concluded that it was impossible to "figure any of it out."

Psychological disorders raised still other complications. Although Greta described herself as suffering from both depression and anxiety, many women rejected the psychological labels assigned to them. Depression, some insisted, was a reasonable response to loss. Anxiety helped to keep them vigilant. After remarking that people frequently described her as "paranoid," Rose Jensen commented, "What's interesting is the origin of the word 'paranoia,' from the Latin means 'heightened anxiety,' and that's actually a good thing. It helps keep you alive. I don't feel like I have the luxury of not being observant. Nobody is going to find my cancer but me." And several survivors charged that doctors were far too quick to assign psychological causes to women's physical complaints.

Despite those various difficulties, we defined women's complaints as posttreatment symptoms whenever the survivors defined them at least partly as such. Table 1.1 demonstrates that the two most common symptoms were also the ones that figure most prominently in recent research: fatigue and cognitive dysfunction. One study found that approximately a third of breast cancer survivors still experience fatigue between one and five years after diagnosis.[9] Because being tired is an inevitable feature of everyday life, many women sought to explain how their experiences were different. "Usually people get tired, and you can work through it," one woman stated. "But now what happens is I'm either fine or I crash totally. And I absolutely cannot work through it. It's like everything shuts down. I get shaky, and it's like my blood pressure drops and my blood sugar, everything, and I have to literally stop and rest or go to bed. . . . I'll be fine, I'll feel great, and then all of a sudden everything just crashes, and I'll go, 'What caused that?' I don't get slightly tired. I get exhausted." Another woman stressed her long recovery time: "When a regular person gets tired, they get tired and they can just sit down. But when I get tired, it will be days before I'm right back again."

Some women emphasized the intensity of their fatigue by contrasting themselves to siblings close to them in age. Ida Jaffe said, "I have three sisters, and we would run and do ten million things in one day. And I'm the one who's like, 'OK, guys, I have to take a break' or 'I have to rest' or 'Let me go take a nap.'" An accountant drew a comparison with her former self: "I used to be a person who could work a twelve-hour day on a routine basis and then go out at night and ride my horse and clean my house. I had a lot of energy." But she could not "do that anymore": "In fact, I have no reserve at all. When I'm exhausted I have to lie down, not just relax for fifteen minutes. I have to come home and sleep."

Women also distinguished posttreatment fatigue by emphasizing its mental component. Greta described herself as "brain exhausted." A teacher said, "at the end of the day I am spent, where before I was energetic. And it's not a physical spent; it's a mental spent that I didn't used to have." Ida Jaffe told a focus group, "If I walk into a mall and go inside, I just become overwhelmed. It's exhausting. It's like it hits you. I actually went with someone over this weekend. She wanted to go to a super Wal-Mart because she wanted to pick up things, and I walked in and I said, 'You know, I'll meet you up front.' They had a little bench and I had to sit there. I was actually falling asleep. She wasn't there that long, half an hour." When another woman commented, "It's like sensory overload," Ida continued,

> You're right, the mall would be like overwhelming. For years, I couldn't walk the entire mall. Fox Hills Mall! And you know, that's not that big. I mean we're talking DelAmo, then we're talking big.

I could not walk into Fox Hills Mall to save my life. I guess within the last maybe three or four years I can go from May Company to J. C. Penny's, but I've got to stop in between and hold on to something. . . . Now God forbid I go to May Company, and based on my size, I've gotta walk down to Lane Bryant. When you get to Lane Bryant, you don't want to try anything on.

Cognitive dysfunction is the other major symptom survivors reported. Colloquially known as "chemobrain," it took various forms, including memory loss and difficulties with both concentration and organization. Researchers using positron emission tomography (PET) scans have demonstrated that chemotherapy can damage the brain, producing results that can last at least ten years.[10] More than any other symptom, chemobrain provoked complaints of frustration. "My mind has diminished drastically," Annie Briggs remarked.

I used to be a very memorable person and not write things down, such as "I need to go to the doctor on Tuesday, the thirty-first of August." As a matter of fact, I told my girlfriend yesterday, "Remind me to call my shrink to see what time I have to go to the doctor on August thirty-first." Little things: "Where did I put my keys?" It's such a mind-boggling thing. I know I have twenty dollars, and I know where I put it. I go there, and it's not there. That is very frustrating. And I don't have a long-term grasp of staying with a book. Maybe eight or ten pages, and I'm irritated, where it used to be where I could do twenty pages.

A bank teller said,

Someone can ask me something, and I try to remember, and I can't. I say, "Just a minute now." Beforehand I'd remember it. Someone asked me, "What do you use on your hair?" and I said, "OK, I'll tell you. I can't think of it now." But before she left the bank I still couldn't tell her. I had to come home and look at the bottle and say, "Oh, there it is. I remember now." But it's too late now. It takes a while for you to remember things. Sometimes I'm driving and I know where I'm going, but I don't know what happens. My mind goes, and I say, "Oh, I was supposed to turn here or there," and I say, "Well, what are you doing? Where are you going? You missed a turn, and you have to go back and everything." I know one time I was just really frustrated because I said, "Where am I? Where am I going? Do you remember? You said you were going to this place. Well, where is the place that you're going? Do you remember? No." I had to sit there and think about it. That's frustrating. And concentrating—that's a problem. I'm trying to focus sometimes, and I'm looking at something on TV and I don't know what's going on. I'm supposed to be watching it, but I don't know what's happening. I'm looking, but I'm not paying attention. My mind is going somewhere else.

When asked whether she had any problem finding the right word, Pat Garland gave this account:

It's right here circling around, and it won't come out. It's a word that you say every other day. And it won't come out of your mouth. It's like you want to scream because you know it but you cannot say it. To save your life you can't say it. What used to really piss me off was movie stars. You're talking about a singer or somebody, and you can't say their name. You've got their record and CDs in your house, and you can't say, "Aretha Franklin." It's here, but you can't say it. I wasn't the greatest speller before, but now the words that I could spell, I can't see them, and I can't visualize how they should be. I don't write anymore. And it's very frustrating to have a conversation.

Yet another woman reported, "I started going to school about the same time as I started my cancer treatment. I'm studying French. And sometimes I get so frustrated. It's almost like when you break a thermometer and the mercury creeps away. I can almost catch it, but I can't quite. It feels so different to me from how I was before."

Like Greta Shaw, most women experienced several complaints simultaneously. The median number was fifteen. The cumulative effect was often more serious than the impact of any particular one. "My worst days are the ones where it would sort of all kind of hit me at once," Nina Worth remarked. "Like I would notice that I couldn't remember a word and that there was something that was making me anxious. And there were days when I had like the chemobrain, the hot flashes, sort of all going at once. And I'm thinking, 'OK, am I just completely falling apart here?'" A second survivor viewed herself as "getting attacked on a lot of different fronts." Treatment for one symptom might be contraindicated for another. And some symptoms interacted. Cognitive dysfunction, for example, intensified Marge Barlow's anxiety and depression, which in turn exacerbated her fatigue.

Another cause of distress was that symptoms rarely followed a predictable pattern of progress and recovery. Just as survivors had expected the end of treatment to signal a return to "normal" life, so they had assumed any lingering side effects would gradually subside and eventually disappear. But severity often waxed and waned. Greta's mouth sore, for example, "comes and goes and gets worse at different times." Anticipating her interview, she had wondered whether she would feel "really foggy" or "pretty clear." When recovery occurred, it often reached a plateau and then halted. "It was really odd," a nurse recalled. "It was like a curtain lifting in February. It was like all of a sudden, I said to my husband, 'I'm back.' He said, 'You're not all the way back, but I can tell you're on your way.' So I'm better, because chemo was like death. But as far as comparing it to where I was before that, I'm not anywhere near where I was or where I'd like to be." Another woman said, "I was off work during the whole treatment, and when I went back to work, oh, I fought being so tired. And I had a nurse that said, 'You'll get back to normal in about six months. It will take you six months.' And I kept going, 'Oh, OK, good, six months I'll be back to my old self.' But I waited and I waited, and I continue to be tired."

Proximity to cancer diagnosis also endowed the symptoms with special significance. As one woman noted, "always in the back of your mind" is the question, "Is this cancer? Is it coming back?" Another survivor described her leg pain as "very, very scary" because "you ask, 'Well, what are the symptoms of recurrence?' and bone pain is one of them, and then you think, 'Oh, my gosh, my leg is really, really aching!'" A third woman said, "I had like a little shock of pain in the area of the breast where I had surgery and the scar. That's the most common place for the breast cancer to return, so it makes me worry. I always have that fear." Cognitive dysfunction frightened a fourth survivor: "I think memory loss, I wonder if I have a tumor in the brain." Yet another woman's breathlessness reminded her of her mother during the months preceding her death from breast cancer:

> Climbing up and down the stairs, I have to rest in between. Yesterday I came up the stairs, and I found myself having to stop part of the way up, and when I came in I immediately sat down. Then I went back and got my little bag of groceries that I had and brought them in the house. I tend to compare myself to her a lot—my mom and her problems. I think it was after the third year that she had the recurrence, and I'm kind of at that point right now too. So I'm thinking about her and her breathing and how she came up the stairs.

Other symptoms felt like scars. A few literally were marks on the body. A woman who had had a double mastectomy reported, "There is always the daily reminder of what I've been through when I look in the mirror. You can never totally forget because this is the result." Another woman included among her list of symptoms several "small things that have affected me physically, like my lower eyelashes didn't come back. Things that are really insignificant but they remind me what I went through. My hair is different after it came back from before I lost it. It's not devastating, but it's just another thing to say, 'Well, it's because I had cancer, I went through all that treatment.'" Invisible symptoms stirred up painful memories for a third survivor. Asked which of her many complaints caused the greatest distress, she answered, "Fatigue, because it reminds me and makes me feel like an invalid. Even though the degenerative joint disease hurts and is painful, the fatigue is worse because it's all over my body. And that reminds me that I had a very devastating treatment, and it reminds me of the cancer."

But symptoms could lose as well as gain significance in cancer's aftermath. Having experienced "the big stuff," Nina Worth viewed all her problems as "little nit-picky stuff." Another survivor was well aware that lymphedema was now a permanent part of her life; nevertheless, it was "something minimal when you think of what could have happened."

Although all the women in this study had experienced breast cancer, their biographies varied dramatically in other ways. Sexual dysfunction disturbed Greta because it caused marital "friction." By contrast, when we asked a single woman about the impact of her diminished libido, she guffawed and then exclaimed, "Show me a good man and it might be a different story." Early menopause was a happy relief to Marge Barlow. She had never wanted children and was glad to be rid of the "hassle." Although roughly the same age, another woman felt "robbed" of something important: "I stopped getting my period just when my daughter started getting hers. There was a part of me that just wanted to experience that female experience with her. Just for us to be able to share that, and I wasn't able to, and that I was sad about. So it extended beyond my relationship with myself in terms of not being able to have children." Because Nina Worth became engaged to be married while undergoing chemotherapy, premature menopause caused special anguish:

> The timing was really just so unfortunate because it took thirty-six years to find the man that I wanted to marry. And everything was like converging; the timing was just bad. I was like, I thought, "OK, so I actually managed to meet this man, fall in love, in the middle of my chemo and radiation, and you are going to tell me at this point that I am now going to have hot flashes and go through early menopause, when, you know, I haven't even gotten married yet?" Because, of course, one of the questions at the beginning with the doctor was, "How do you feel about children before we start talking about chemo? Is that an issue?" And I'm like, "Well, you know, there's frankly no one in sight, so no, it's not an issue. We need to do all the things that you think I need to do to prevent a recurrence." And it was sort of, "OK, you could go through early menopause," and I was like, "Yeah, yeah, yeah. I understood all that, that all those things could happen," but at the time it wasn't really bothering me so much. But it's bothered me a whole lot more with Tom in the picture and thinking, you know, "You can't do this to me now." After all this, that just didn't seem right.

Symptoms that undermined self-esteem also inflicted deep wounds. Thus, severe and persistent fatigue was especially difficult for women who had prided themselves on unusually high energy levels. "I worked two forty-hour jobs before I got sick," Annie Briggs told us. "Eight hours on both, and sometimes overtime on both. I don't have what I used to have. I'm not what I used to be." Mastectomies provoked exceptionally sharp grief in three women. "It's been a great personal loss to me," one remarked sixteen years after the removal of her breast. "I think I could have lost something else on my body, but losing a breast was the identification of me. This is who I am. I related that as being part of my personality, and losing it [meant] they were taking away something of who I was." A former model, Jean Trawick said, "I was looking through a portfolio from when I was in my late twenties, and there is a picture of me on the beach with a very lightweight swimsuit, and you can see my breasts. I miss that. I miss not having my body." The third commented, "I was a cleavage person. I showed it. I loved it. But everything I wear is turtlenecks now."

When self-image had been tied to mental abilities, cognitive impairments devastated survivors. Engineer Rose Jensen had never considered herself "a good dancer, singer, or particularly pretty." Her self-confidence had rested on her exceptional memory, but that was now gone. A writer complained, "I don't really have access to words as I used to. I have found that really annoying. I hate it, and it makes me angry. I'm very good with names, but the names won't come as quickly. I mean, not all the time, but sometimes I can see it hanging there but I just can't touch it. When it happens I feel incredibly inarticulate, and I'm someone who has always been able to express myself. So it's very hard because it starts to become a question of identity." A former nurse said,

> I went through disability testing through the community college and was found to have auditory cognitive processing which is two levels lower than the norm and also short-term memory retrieval two levels below average. And they said, "Otherwise with everything you perform normal." However, I think that the problem was before I performed extremely high. And that was a frustration. People would go, "Well, you're average." And I'd stare at them and go,

"You don't understand. I may be average now, but this is *not* who I was before." And this is really hard to get used to.

Finally, symptoms acquired meaning from the culture in which they were experienced. The glorification of high energy magnified the impact of long-term fatigue. The cultural fixation on large breasts amplified the effect of mastectomies.[11] And the widespread belief that people can overcome all troubles endowed all chronic illness and disability with especially negative connotations. Comparing themselves to breast cancer survivors who had completely recovered, the women in our study judged themselves harshly. As a result, we will see, many refrained from seeking the social support they wanted at home and demanding essential accommodations at work.

"Who Am I?"

A major theme in breast cancer narratives is a sense of radical alteration. Although women often assume familiar patterns of life will resume as soon as chemotherapy and radiation end, most still feel profoundly transformed long afterward. Surveying the large literature of personal writings on the disease, one observer notes that virtually all wrestle with the question, "Who am I now that I am a person with breast cancer?"[12] To some extent, that question derives from the trauma of diagnosis and treatment as well as from the aftereffects medical experts have long acknowledged: breast loss, lymphedema, premature menopause, and the constant awareness that a terrifying disease has struck and can return at any time. Lingering symptoms that have received less attention may make identity issues even more urgent. The two most prevalent complaints, fatigue and cognitive impairment, shatter valued sources of personal esteem. We will see that those symptoms also force many women to reconstruct self-images by disrupting work, leisure activities, and key social relationships.

Medical sociologists and anthropologists remind us that symptoms derive meaning from sufferers' individual lives. "Acting like a sponge," Arthur Kleinman writes, "illness soaks up personal and social significance form the world of the sick person."[13] We have seen that fatigue was especially devastating to women who previously had enjoyed high energy levels, that cognitive impairment had the greatest salience for those who defined themselves in terms of their mental abilities, and that a desire for children accentuated the anguish of premature menopause. The subsequent chapters demonstrate how the responses of friends, family members, lovers, physicians, and employers further shape survivors' understandings of their ongoing problems.

2

"We Saved Your Life.
Now Leave Us the Hell Alone"

PAT GARLAND HAS little good to say about any of the doctors she saw either during or after cancer. When we interviewed her in her small studio apartment, eleven years had elapsed since she learned that a breast lump was malignant. Nevertheless, she vividly recalled that moment:

> To start out, it's not routine, but they treat it as routine. I remember when I was diagnosed, and the doctor told me that I had breast cancer that afternoon. And when I stood up my legs went out from under me; they were wobbly. He said, "Oh, you're having a terrible reaction." Duh! He didn't know what to do! You just told me I have cancer! My mother had it, so now I'm thinking that she died from it—yeah, my legs went a little weak. What did they think people did when you tell them they have cancer? Ignoring the fact that it took you three months to tell me that. We won't even talk about how long it took them to diagnose me. My tumor ran from my nipple to my chest. And I went from November until January 31 before they, on January 31, told me that I had breast cancer.

Other complaints focused on the period after chemotherapy ended. A drug prescribed to alleviate Pat's hot flashes led to peripheral neuropathy, a condition that can cause tingling, numbness, and pain in the hands and feet:

My hands do not work. At the very beginning after chemotherapy I couldn't hold a cup. I couldn't assure myself that I wouldn't drop it. That's how bad my hands were. But in order to diagnose what was wrong with me, they did what they call a nerve damage test. And as everyone knows, you're not supposed to stick needles into your surgical arm. And of course this test involved needles. So what was extremely humorous today, but not then, was that after they did this test, my arm and hands swoll up. And I ran around Kaiser this particular day after I couldn't figure out what was wrong, and when it swoll up I couldn't fold my hand and make a fist. I couldn't clap my hands in church. I couldn't do any of the simplistic things in life. So I said, "You better go and ask what's going on." And I went in, and it took three doctors and one standing in a hallway to tell me that I had lymphedema.

Pat's immediate concern now was to treat the lymphedema, but she also had to find the cause of the nerve damage: "Because CMF[1] does not cause peripheral neuropathy, everybody made me think that nothing was happening, that it was all in my head, that the pain and the fingers were not working." To counter her self-doubt, she turned elsewhere for medical information:

My girlfriend and I, we started researching, because my hands got more and more like they were paralyzed. I would have to have occasions where my friends would have to undress me. So we figured out, my girlfriend and I in the PDR book,[2] that the drug can cause nerve damage. So we went to the oncologist, who happened to be on vacation, so we got his substitute and we showed it to him in the PDR book, because the nurses didn't believe us. So we told him to drag out a PDR, to get one, and we'll find it for you. So we did, and immediately the substitute doctor took me off the drug.

Another doctor proposed an equally inappropriate therapy for her menopausal symptoms:

The gynecologist, he was an older guy, a white guy. And I was trying to tell him, you know, how severe the mood swings and the hot flashes were and how miserable this was making me feel. And he was like, "What's the problem? Why can't you take estrogen?" And I said, "I'm a breast cancer survivor." And he said, "Is that a problem? You need to be on HRT."[3] And I'm like, "No! I don't think that's a good idea."

A support group helped Pat make sense of the memory loss she experienced after chemotherapy: "At first it was just I was losing my mind. But understanding those things, and having a place to put it where you could resolve it, put closure to it. I learned about it by talking to other breast cancer survivors. None of us could remember. We validated each other."

For years, however, she was unable to get a diagnosis for joint pain, her most debilitating symptom:

I was on a cane. I was going to the doctor for the pain in my back and the pain in my knees. . . . What was so awful about it, there was *no* validation, none. . . . That is what makes it so hard, because I will sit here and hurt for weeks before I go in because I was— because every time I would go in at the beginning they would tell me I had cancer. And they would only look for and give me cancer-related tests. . . . I wanted him to look for something else to diagnose me with. All he would do is sit there and write down my symptoms and then say, "OK, bone scan." He gave me cancer-related tests. He never looked for any other things. . . . And the general practitioner that was supposed to be involved with my case, I came in one day with my cane and I'm sitting here thinking that she was going to give me some info about why I was hurting. Why was I in so much pain? And she said, "You know, you don't have cancer." Her response to me was, "You need to get back out there and get back to life." In other words I was moaning and groaning, and as far as she was concerned, what was the big deal? . . . The medical community stressed me, and then they would turn around and tell me that I wasn't handling the cancer diagnosis. It's not in my head today that I can't stir to go make some cornbread or to whip up some eggs. They're sort of like, "OK, we caught it in time. We saved your life. Now leave us the hell alone." That's how I feel. They saved my life, but then the value of my life after they saved it with the chemotherapy was zero.

Significantly, without a diagnostic label for her symptoms, when Pat left her job, she could not claim benefits from Social Security Disability, a federal insurance program that provides payment to disabled people who are unable to work. She might have been eligible for benefits, but only if a physician certified her inability to work. "The doctors kept saying, 'You're going to get better.' They said breast cancer was not debilitating. They said it had a good prognosis as far as living was concerned. So I'm always trying to figure out how I'm going to pay my rent and take care of my sixteen-year-old."

A close friend stopped believing Pat's complaints:

It wasn't really anything hurting which you could pinpoint, tell somebody my throat is hurting or my thigh is hurting. I was just sick as a dog. And my girlfriend said, "You know, the last thing I want to hear is you telling me you are sick and you can't specify what's wrong with you." So I was learning then don't talk to people. Keep it to yourself.

Occasionally, she "told lies": "'What's wrong with you?' 'Oh, I was in a car accident!' Because it was easier, and they could understand that. You have to give people something that they could relate to."

She urged us to educate doctors:

I think one area the medical community really needs to look at is preparing the patients long-term. They really need to do a better job. Yes, you've got cancer, you need to get it out, and you're moving forwards with that and you'll have this and you'll have that and you know they know the treatment and I looked it up myself and I had a second opinion, I did all those things. But not in any of the reviews did anyone talk about how you would feel after. I would have prepared differently. I would have made more of a change in my life then.

Asked what she wished doctors had said to her when she first be-gan experiencing pain, she had no difficulty answering: "'It's a real thing, the condition exists. . . . this is something that you may have to go through that we can't treat. We can't fix it right away, but we're going to go through it together. We're not going to send you home thinking that it's just you.'"

Patients and Doctors

The balance of power between physicians and patients has shifted dra-matically since the 1970s.[4] A major impetus for that transformation was the women's health movement. Although activists initially fo-cused on reproductive issues, they gradually expanded their purview to challenge medical hegemony over breast cancer treatment in two ways. First, they intervened in debates about the Halsted radical mas-tectomy; as we noted in the introduction, that surgery caused major deformities in the chest area. Feminists branded it an assault against women and touted the advantages of less aggressive therapies. Second, they demanded an end to the so-called one-step procedure, in which a mastectomy was performed while a woman was still anesthetized if the pathology report on the biopsied tumor indicated a malignancy. As women activists argued, that procedure deprived patients of the right to choose whether or not to have a mastectomy. Partly as a re-sult of feminist agitation, doctors gradually abandoned both the radi-cal mastectomy and the one-step procedure.[5] Summarizing the impact of the women's health movement, one historian concludes that "the interaction between physician and patient—and especially between male surgeon and woman patient—would never be the same."[6]

Like numerous other researchers, we found that African Ameri-can women were less likely than white women to surrender to medi-cal authority.[7] Although Pat told a story of unusual medical negligence and incompetence, the hostility and suspiciousness she expressed were widespread among the African Americans in our study. One explanation for those attitudes is the long history of medical exploitation of black bodies, beginning during slavery and continuing through the Tuskegee syphilis study.[8] Another is the underrepresentation of blacks among health professionals.[9] Although many of the African American women we interviewed said they might have related better to members of their own race, they had had no option but to consult white physicians.[10] Further, seven white women (but only one black woman) had physician relatives who had been able to intercede for them, explain medical information, and help them forge more egalitarian relationships with other doctors. Some evidence suggests that a patient's race influences the type of care doctors deliver. For example, a study of communication patterns between breast cancer patients and oncologists found that physicians provide more information to white patients than to members of racial and ethnic minorities.[11] The higher education level of the white women we interviewed similarly stood them in good stead. The same study reported that patients with more than a high school education receive more medical information than those with less schooling.[12] And some African Americans we spoke to obtained care in relatively undesirable settings. Pat was convinced that she would have been treated far better at one of the two major university cancer centers in Los Angeles than at the hospital to which her health plan assigned her. Two African American women in our study (but no white women) lacked any form of health insurance at the time of diagnosis and thus had attended the hospitals and clinics operated by the Los Angeles County Department of Health Services, notorious for their long waiting lists, severe overcrowding, and impersonality.

Despite the many differences between the African American and white women, they typically agreed about the ways cancer affected their relationships to the medical profession.[13] Some members of both groups recalled that the diagnosis initially increased respect for doctors. Feelings of extreme vulnerability encouraged them to place their faith in the certainty of science and to endow physicians with almost miraculous powers. Lack of clarity about the best course of action had the same effect. Was a mastectomy appropriate? If so, should it be followed by reconstruction? What kind? Were radiation and chemotherapy necessary? When should they begin? Which protocol was right? An accountant remembered being overwhelmed by the massive amount of information she was expected to absorb and the strange language in which it was couched:

Doctors would explain something to me, and they'd say, "Do you get it?" Well, you are so shocked and so terrified and it seems so fast [that doctors suggest] these harsh treatments that you say, "Yeah, I guess." But there are different types of chemotherapy, different types of side effects, percentages of what will give you the disease-free survival. Even these words, "disease-free survival," that's not a normal part of one's vocabulary. It's not like "tomato" and "mayonnaise." You know, what is "disease-free survival" or "time to relapse"? What is a "relapse"?

Not surprisingly, some women sought one authority they could unambiguously trust. A survivor recalled, "Early on I said to the radiologist that I'm not sure I made the right decision about lumpectomy as opposed to the mastectomy, and he said, 'There was absolutely no reason for you to have a mastectomy.' And I really had to hang on to that and believe him." Ida Jaffe told us, "When you're going into it, you're trusting these people and feel that your life is in their hands. You believe every word that they tell you." Years later, some women still spoke reverently of their physicians. One commented,

The man who was with me for many years went off to do research and gave up his practice. . . . I don't know what he's doing. I feel connected to him to this day. If I saw him, I would engage in a conversation and I'd listen to him because he saved my life, and I will be connected to him all my days. And I go to his practice regardless. It cost me three, four, five hundred dollars last time, but I'm going and I'm going to spend whatever it takes so that I'm there, because they do a very thorough job. And I'm able to ask what happened to Dr. T.

But the events surrounding diagnosis were more likely to undermine confidence than foster it. Diagnostic errors are far more common than generally realized, occurring in 10 to 15 percent of cases.[14] Mammograms are easily misread.[15] Nine of the women in our study (including Pat Garland) charged that doctors initially had missed their cancers, often with serious repercussions. One said,

When I first noticed something was different, I was scratching my breast and it was turning real red and flaming hot. So I went to the emergency room, and they told me it was very common and they gave me some antibiotics and told me to take the antibiotics for ten days. And then I took them for the ten days, and then they told me to get another mammogram because I had just had a mammogram about three months before. So when I got the mammogram they called me back; the doctor told me, "There is a mass." So I went to the surgeon, and the surgeon looked at the mammogram or the pictures and she said, "I think you just had an overzealous radiologist. I don't believe you have breast cancer." So I waited six months. I knew nothing about breast cancer, so I waited six months. And when I went back they did another mammogram, and they found it. . . . When they did the surgery, they found three positive lymph nodes, and to this day I believe that had they done that six months before then I wouldn't have had them.

Another woman explained why she withdrew her trust: "I had the cancer, and I was misdiagnosed for two years. In retrospect, it was on my mammogram, but it was not read correctly. So this attitude of 'don't worry about it; I'll worry about it' doesn't cut the mustard for me. I'm very paranoid right now. And when someone tells me, 'don't worry about it,' I'll start doing my own research."

Six other women suddenly realized that a long-term therapy previously endorsed by medical experts may have caused harm. Throughout the 1990s, doctors routinely recommended that women take hormone replacement therapy (HRT) at the first sign of menopause and continue the regime for the rest of their lives to prevent osteoporosis and heart disease and counter menopausal symptoms, including hot flashes, sleeplessness, and depression. Since then, medical advice has changed back and forth. In 2002, the Women's Health Initiative study of twenty-five thousand postmenopausal women reported that HRT not only increased the risk of several serious diseases (including breast cancer) but also failed to stave off heart problems.[16] Researchers who continued to study the data concluded in 2007 that the therapy was safe if inaugurated soon after menopause.[17] Even before the publication of those conflicting reports, however, some experts had begun to point to a link between HRT and breast cancer.[18] Thus, although the women we interviewed typically had received their diagnoses before 2002, they would have been instructed to cease use of the drug immediately. One stated,

> The day I was diagnosed they told me to stop taking hormone replacement therapy, and when I did and nothing happened, it gave me a deeper sense that I didn't need the damn things in the first place. I wasn't suffering. But I trusted the doctors that were treating me, and they were each telling me, "I have my wife on this too. I believe it's the right thing to do." Their wives were about my age. I respected them. One of the things I really fault about the medical profession is nobody checked my estrogen level, and I didn't know enough to say, "Why are you giving me this without checking if my estrogen level indicates that I need more." . . . I was not a doctor, and I didn't know how to put all this information together. And that's why I need to know as much as I can, because I don't want to be told. I want to ask, and I want it explained to me. . . . Instead of the experience I had with the hormone replacement therapy and saying, "Yes, doctor, if you really insist, I'll do it," because I didn't know how to argue my way out of it.

As a result of learning that hormone replacement therapy might have "triggered" her cancer, another woman became "more skeptical" than before: "I don't accept everything that they tell you. I'm willing to look into alternatives and seek second and third and fourth advice."

Many women did not need such evidence of physician fallibility to convince them to remain actively involved in medical decisions. The explosion of information about breast cancer on the Internet and in print enabled several to consider themselves experts. Like Pat, one woman felt competent to consult medical literature:

> I did research, and I went to libraries, medical research libraries, and hospital libraries, and all of a sudden I felt that I knew more than everybody, and I could manage my care and I could discuss my care with my doctor when they wanted to do something that I didn't

think was a good idea. I could back it up with a journal article, and we could have a conversation. They would roll their eyes and think, "Oh my, she's been doing research, reading again." But they talked to me, and nothing was ever done that I didn't understand.

Moreover, patients who turn to either the Internet or printed medical material repeatedly receive advice urging them to consider themselves partners of physicians. The women in our study who had been able to "shop" for doctors selected those willing to share knowledge. "I love my oncologist," Tessa McKnight commented.

> I interviewed another oncologist before, because I read somewhere it's gonna be a long relationship; you gotta connect with them. So everyone was sure that I was gonna love this woman oncologist in Century City; she was just like the best. And I was like, "Oh, OK." So I went to her, and . . . I did not connect with her at all. It seemed like she's been in this business too long, and she's treating me just like another number and a statistic, and I just can't work with that. And then someone else had suggested P.B., and I went to him, and he took like two hours with me and explained. I had all these [questions]. Cancer's so obscure, and I hadn't had any experience with it at all. I really wanted to understand about the cells and whatnot. And he just was making diagrams for me, and he spent all this time with me.

Although Tessa's preferred doctor was a man, several survivors assumed female physicians would be more willing to establish egalitarian relationships.[19] One woman explained why she did not go back to the doctor she had consulted (during her first bout with breast cancer in 1994) when the disease returned six years later:

> I think I had to get more assertive with cancer. I had a certain oncologist who was a real sweet man. He was very nurturing and very warm. But he was the kind of guy, he was great for great-grandma, who just said, "Do whatever you have to do to fix me. I'm not asking that many questions." So I went in, and the first time it was fine

because I didn't really ask a lot of questions. I just, you know, this is the way it is, this is what you do, and all is fine. The second time I went in and I saw him, he said, "We are going to put you on some chemo, see if it responds. If it responds, we are going to talk about a bone marrow transplant." And I went and I did some reading about bone marrow transplants, and they weren't looking as effective as they thought. And I thought, "Well why would you want to go through that if it's not that good?" I went in and started asking questions, and he said, "Woman, I am trying to save your life. Just listen to me." And that was the last appointment I had with him. I found a new oncologist.

A trip to Iowa had bolstered this woman's determination to make a change:

My cousin was working for the bone marrow transplant for the University of Iowa, and she says, "Come back here and I'm going to have my boss talk to you." So I went, and the head of the clinic there sat down with me for an hour and treated me like I knew something about statistics. And I said, "I understand statistics. If you have a 15 percent chance of survival, it doesn't mean you are not one of the fifteen. It means that if you have one hundred spaces and you toss a coin, fifteen of them will . . . And I understand that idea; it's probability, it's chance." I said, "I want some real information here because I need to make decisions." And he was really good, and I said, "OK, now tell me: What is the long-term average survival rate for this treatment, that treatment, that treatment?" It was like one month or two months difference. I kind of thought in my head, "Well why on earth would anyone want to do that if they are only going to increase their odds so much on average?" So I went back and I felt like, you know, somebody.

Armed with her new information, she found physicians who were willing to cede authority: "I went down to Kaiser, and I went into the office and I said, 'Is there another oncologist here? Do you have a female?' And they had just hired a woman, and she was excellent, and I had her until she left to go to Minnesota. And I got another woman that's great, let's me help make decisions, and [says], 'What do you think about this?'"

Although this woman did not tell us why her attitude changed so dramatically, we can speculate that both the recurrence and the aggressiveness of the treatment her doctor prescribed in 2000 led her to reassess the trust she previously had placed in him. Shifting popular understandings of the role of physicians also must have had an impact. As a survivor, she would have been especially likely to watch the rise of a new breast cancer movement during the 1990s, challenging patients' deference to medical expertise and demanding their active participation in all aspects of their care.[20]

Women who either considered doctors less responsive than expected or had no choice but to settle for the ones assigned by health care plans employed various strategies to assert control. Several brought family members to appointments. One, for example, said, "Before, when I went by myself, he was inconsistent with his answers, and that was a problem. I thought because I was under so many different medications and also emotionally that I'm not hearing what's going on. He realized that I like to bring people in, and our communication changed, and he's being responsive to me. When someone was with me he was much better. And at least I knew that we're both hearing the same thing." Frustrated by her inability to obtain adequate information during a standard fifteen-minute office visit, one patient "would call up and get a half-hour consultation": "Then I'd walk in and say, 'I have a half an hour,' and I would go sit down and put my watch on the counter." Following the advice of a friend, Marsha Dixler prepared questions beforehand:

> When I would leave Dr. O.'s office I would be in tears at the way he treated me. Deirdre [a support group leader] told me, "You have the right to speak up, to ask questions, the right to tell him you don't want to do that. You don't have to take everything that he says. It should be a doctor and patient agreement." I did not know that. From her I learned to speak, read. When I go to the doctor I'm ready, I have my questions. I usually type up questions.

I try to be understanding and considerate because I'm not your only patient. "If you can't answer all my questions, take it home. Answer it and get back to me. But I want all five of those questions on that paper."

Realizing that her doctor failed to perceive her as "an individual," Marsha dyed her hair: "so he can look at me. Whatever you have to do to make your doctor notice you, then that's what you do."

The emergence of long-term, posttreatment problems provoked new challenges to medical authority. Like the revelations about hormone replacement therapy, the symptoms served as powerful reminders that medicine could harm as well as heal. A few survivors began to reconsider the original therapeutic decision. As her fatigue went "on and on and on and on," one woman started "wondering if the radiation was really necessary," because "the cancer I had was the best kind." Another woman questioned the type of chemotherapy administered: "I've read things and heard several people say that they overtreat us as far as the chemo because they'd rather be overaggressive than be underaggressive."

Most survivors, however, had a tremendous stake in believing they had received appropriate therapy. Rather than reassessing treatment decisions, they complained about the inadequacy of the information doctors had provided. Although no woman charged physicians with failure to obtain informed consent, several insisted that they should have been warned about the possibility of long-term consequences. "I'm trying my best to be positive," one stated,

> but I've been disappointed that I went through the process that the doctors told me to go through. You know, these were the options, I needed to make the decision, I did the research, I consulted different physicians as well. But no one ever told me that when chemo was done, radiation was done, I would feel this way. . . . So I think the biggest piece is yes, there's this, what the doctors call a plan for treatment or therapy. And it's wonderful, apparently, it's working, and I'm confident it's going to work, but they just don't tell you what all of this is really about. I feel very cheated.

A second woman noted, "Physically I think that I have been somewhat fortunate except that I have chronic pain where the radiation was, in my whole chest. I will say something to my doctor, and he is like, 'Oh yeah,' and I say, 'Is it ever going to go away? Just be honest,' and he says, 'Um, no.' And I was like, 'OK, well, it was nice of you to tell me now that I'm eight years out. That's fine.'"

Lacking prior information, Ida Jaffe had been unable to take precautions:

> I did not get lymphedema right away, and I didn't know anything about lymphedema until it happened. About a year after my treatment, one morning I woke up and my hand was swollen, and I was like, "Wow, what is this?" It scared me, so I called the doctor and went in. Of course, they diagnosed it as lymphedema. I don't think they tell you enough about it to prevent it, because at that time I was carrying a purse. Maybe not such a big purse because my right side was tender, but had I known that possibly I could have gotten lymphedema from wearing the purse, picking up heavy things and things like that, I would have been more careful about it, and that could have been prevented.

Like Pat Garland, this woman might have made major life changes:

> I wish my doctor had said, especially with the Adriamycin, "You could have some cognitive issues," because I have a very stressful job. In fact, I am out on leave right now because it's been building. I think if my doctor told me, I might have at the time rethought or reevaluated whether I wanted to go back. I might have decided to go ahead and stay out on disability for a while and rethink what I wanted to do with my life. Because now I find I am just totally burned out.

One reason these women may have received so little counseling about the possibility of long-term symptoms is that the doctors may have assumed their primary task was to provide reassurance during a particularly anxious period. Another reason may be that little information about those symptoms was available when most women in this study began treatment. But the survivors' complaints also point to a widespread problem in physician communication. One recent study found that doctors convey information about the adverse side effects of the new medications they prescribe only one-third of the time.[21]

After symptoms arose, women consulted not just their surgeons, radiologists, and oncologists but also general practitioners and a wide assortment of other specialists. Most of the criticisms of doctors, however, focused on those who had treated the cancer. Anticipating negative reactions, a few women refrained even from bringing their symptoms to physician attention. One said, "I haven't discussed with the oncologist the memory—the continual memory thing—or the neck. So he hasn't said, 'No, it can't be.' I don't want to burst that bubble because I really thought he was a great guy, is a great guy." Another thought the relationship she had forged with the entire office staff could not withstand any disclosure of long-term problems:

> After the treatment they seem to be always happy to see me because I'm not taking the treatment anymore and I don't have a lot of complaints. And they always tell me I look good. I'll put on makeup and stuff, and, you know, it makes me feel good. So they have more of a positive, good attitude towards me. Before, everyone was working with me and giving me the treatment, they all seemed kind of worried. And now since they don't find cancer, they, you know, "Oh, hi, Ms. A.!" It just seems like they like to see me all the time. It makes me feel good.

Reporting new difficulties, this woman feared, might cause the office to withdraw that welcome. (She may not have been wrong: one social psychologist found that doctors respond more favorably to their healthier patients.)[22] Other women assumed that doctors would either have little knowledge about remedies or prescribe medication that might cause additional difficulties.

But there also were powerful motivations to present the symptoms, and most women did so. The most pressing goal was to gain reassurance.

As already noted, such complaints as headaches and back pain might indicate a host of serious conditions, including a cancer recurrence. Cognitive impairment could be a sign of dementia or mental illness. Once such dire prospects had been eliminated, women wanted doctors to confirm the existence of the symptoms. Soon after discussing cognitive problems with a friend, Marge Barlow had an appointment with her oncologist:

> I started to mention this conversation with the nurse, and she just interrupted me and said, "Oh, chemobrain." She goes, "Yeah, everybody gets that." And I said, "Well, what are you talking about?" And then once she started talking to me about that, then I felt OK: "OK, this is something that other people share." I didn't feel like I was going crazy or a sense of isolation about it or anything. And then the doctor came in, and we talked about it again. And we talk about it now when I go in. It's not an area that medicine is arguing, does this exist or not. So I don't feel like I have one of those illnesses like chronic fatigue: "Is that a real disease?" I don't worry about that at all.

But Marge's experience was highly unusual. Validation rarely came so easily or so quickly. As noted, few studies of the aftereffects of cancer had been published when the majority of survivors in this study underwent treatment. Many thus faced the same dilemma as sufferers of various "contested" diseases, who go from doctor to doctor for years, seeking one who can confirm the complaints. It is easy to understand why few suspend the quest. "The cognitive and social authority of medicine," a sociologist writes,

> includes the power to confirm or deny the reality of everyone's bodily experience. Thus medicine can undermine our belief in ourselves as knowers, since it can cast authoritative doubt on some of our most powerful, immediate experiences, unless they are confirmed by authorized medical descriptions. Moreover, this power of medicine also subjects us to possible private and public invalidation by others—invalidation as knowers and as truth-tellers.[23]

Pat Garland's account illustrates the consequences of that "private and public invalidation." Refusing to believe she remained unwell, Pat's closest friend withdrew her support. Even worse, Pat could not claim benefits from the Social Security Disability Insurance program. As a political scientist argues, "medical certification" is "the core administrative mechanism for a variety of redistributive policies."[24] Doctors are the gatekeepers. Because a breast cancer diagnosis did not qualify Pat for Social Security, she needed her physician to confirm that another health problem prevented her from working. That, however, he refused to do. In addition, the more that doctors viewed Pat as a malingerer, the more she too began to wonder whether her symptoms actually existed.

And yet the power of medicine to define survivors' reality was hardly unlimited. Just as some women remained active participants in their care throughout the treatment process, so some continued to trust their embodied knowledge even in the face of medical skepticism. "I'm very sorry," one said, "you cannot tell me that I'm the first person in the world with all these complaints. And you're not going to tell me that it is my imagination. No, I can't believe that I'm the only one out there going through all this." After noting that doctors could not tell her why her back hurt, "where it does and when it does," another woman added, "but I know how I feel." When a neurologist told a third survivor that the headaches she experienced could not possibly stem from chemotherapy, she refused to return for a follow-up visit: "I've known my body for forty-six years. I can't believe him if he doesn't believe me."

The testimony of other survivors helped to strengthen confidence in the women's experiences.[25] "The support group was where I found out that my symptoms were similar to many other people," a woman remarked. "Before then, just meeting with the doctors, I had the sense that it was just me." Members of Pat's group restored her faith in her sanity: "We validated each other." Leanne Thomas had a similar experience: "When you find another woman that has the same problem, you don't feel as bad. Before, I would tell my shrink, 'I feel like I'm going crazy.' So she suggested that when you're going to the group, listen to hear any of those symptoms from other women. And she made a good suggestion, because when women started talking about it, I didn't feel so bad." Ida Jaffe explained how she learned to take her memory loss seriously:

> It's something that doctors don't really tell you, and in fact they dis-
> courage you from thinking that this is happening to you. They say,
> "Maybe your age," or something like that. When I talked to a young
> lady who was twenty-eight years old, she said, "I just went back to
> work, and I can't even remember my job." That let me know that
> it wasn't just me and it was actually something that has happened
> during the process of chemo or radiation. Where it started I don't
> know, but it's a real symptom.

For another woman, the "best part" of support group meetings was when she found "a connection" between her symptoms and those of others. "It's like, 'Oh, OK, it's not me. It was the treatment.'"

We had the opportunity to witness similar discoveries being made in a focus group conducted with African American women. After listening to a conversation about memory loss, a woman commented, "They told me this was just old age, but now I'm hearing that it's not." Another participant was "glad to hear" the discussion because she "was really feeling like a lone ranger." When the talk turned to shoulder pain, a third woman said, "I'm just so glad you mentioned it because I have it and no one would acknowledge it. They told me I had fibromyalgia." Later, yet another woman remarked, "Doctors make you think you're OK now. . . . Like when you was talking about the vagina being dry, they didn't tell me nothing about that. I learned from other people, much more than I've gotten from the doctors." Emboldened by the accounts of other survivors, the members of this group were able to reject some medical pronouncements and give credence to their own perceptions and feelings.

Nevertheless, very few women could discount medical expertise entirely.[26] For six years Greta Shaw consulted a wide variety of doctors about her mouth problem:

> I can't even tell you how many times I've been to the doctor in the
> past few years. It's ridiculous. I can't remember all of them. I told

my oncologist, of course, thinking that my oncologist would have some kind of insight and really didn't. And actually I've talked to more than one oncologist, just for some kind of glimmer. They just don't seem to know enough about that part of it. I saw an oral surgeon and my dentist, of course. Who else? I saw my dermatologist, another dermatologist, and finally this dermatologist that sent me information on burning tongue syndrome from a doctor at the Mayo Clinic. He was really describing my mouth, and I literally was crying when I read that article. I felt like someone validated it. It took way too long for someone to come up with that, to show me that, I think.

Despite her anger at the length of time it took to receive confirmation, Greta never doubted that doctors alone could dispense it. Like Pat, she urged us to educate the medical community. Doctors need to be able to "tell people that this is something that can happen. They really should know, and it's not like it's going to change anything, but so you don't feel like you're crazy." And she beseeched us to tell her if we ever encountered another doctor who could confirm that her problem was "real."

Another woman similarly craved a medical stamp of legitimacy, even while trusting the knowledge she received through her body. She recalled her last meeting with her oncologist, three months before we interviewed her and eighteen months after she finished treatment: "We were chatting, and I said to him, 'Oh, I forgot.' And he said, 'Oh, that's the chemo.' And I said, 'Ah ha! I caught you!' It was the first time in a year and a half that he had actually acknowledged that the chemo affects your brain." When we asked how his admission affected her, she responded, "Vindicated. Because I knew my body. I knew that I was much more forgetful than I ever was, and I don't think it would have been this enhanced just by age. And what I had been sharing, and not so much complaining about but expressing concerns about, was finally acknowledged by my oncologist." This survivor both "knew" her body and demanded that her doctor ratify its complaints.

Because we interviewed women only once, we could not determine how their attitudes shifted over time. It is likely that many switched back and forth between different positions—sometimes questioning their own sensations, sometimes discrediting the medical profession, and sometimes simultaneously trusting their embodied knowledge and searching for a doctor to validate it.

Although some women would have been satisfied with medical labels, others expected answers to various questions: Would symptoms diminish over time? get worse? remain the same? Unable to learn from her doctors whether the pain and swelling in her breasts would continue, Leanne Thomas asked members of her support group:

> I feel like, "OK, are my breasts ever going to be the same?" I was talking to one lady in the support group, and she goes, "No." I said, "Really?" I said, "No, it's not? I'm thinking it's going to get back to normal." I said, "It hurts." She goes, "It's going to do that." I said, "But they said it's going to stop." She says, "It's not going to stop, honey." I didn't like what I was hearing, but I had to accept it: this is the way it's going to be.

Women were even more disappointed to discover that doctors knew little about possible remedies. When Rose Jensen reported her severe hot flashes, her oncologists "didn't really have information that they could give me, and they'd sit there and throw out things like, 'Well, try black cohosh' [an herbal remedy] or something like that." Another woman explained why she dubbed her physician "not helpful": "When I told my oncologist I was having [sexual] problems, he said, 'You have to have sex more often.' I said, 'Thanks a lot.' I thought he was going to volunteer, but that's not it. . . . I don't have time to talk with people who won't listen."

Two women with lymphedema were especially irate. Lymphedema is a painful and potentially serious side effect of breast cancer surgery, causing swelling of the arms and affecting between 30 and 40 percent of survivors. Treatment typically involves light exercises, wrapping the arm in bandages, massage, and wearing special compression sleeves. Those methods can be effective but only if inaugurated soon after symptoms develop.[27] Ida Jaffe recalled a conversation with her oncologist: "When I talked about the lymphedema, he told me, 'Well you've got to soak [the arm] in warm water.' I stopped by to chat with the nurse, and thank goodness she was there." Hearing the doctor's recommendation, the nurse exclaimed, "Oh no, no, no, no, no! NO!" Another woman was in New York when her arm began to swell. "I had an appointment with my oncologist like a day or two after I came back. I showed him my arm, and he said, 'Oh, you've got lymphedema.' I said, 'Yes, what do you think? Well, what can I do about it?' He said, 'Well, keep your arm up, don't eat salt, and get a sleeve and go on the Internet. There's some places where you can look things up.'" When we asked if her doctor did not have specific resources, she responded,

> Nothing! Nothing! I wanted to kill him. He's a surgeon who does a lot of breast operations. In fact, he's now at [a major] breast center. I mean it was six years ago, but you know, I just was furious, and I said to him, "I've already looked it up on the computer, and I know what you're talking about, and, you know, thanks a lot." He said, "Well maybe the secretary has some stuff on it," and I went to her, and she had like ten-year-old information. So I said, "Well, when I get it, I'll bring you stuff." I felt ridiculous having to tell the doctor.

The one suggestion many doctors made for various symptoms was to try some form of medication, but most women were loath to follow that advice. Several said they were opposed to drugs in general and had made an exception for chemotherapy only after having been convinced it was absolutely essential. Others objected to the particular medication doctors prescribed. One, for example, hesitated to try Celebrex for pain: "I have a daughter who is a pre-med student, and she can pull up on the Internet all of the symptoms for the different medications, and I just didn't like the reading of it, so I haven't taken it."

Breast cancer had often heightened suspicion of medication. "The joint pain is something that I suffer with every day," Ida Jaffe remarked. "I don't take anything for it, because after cancer you don't want to start popping things in your mouth all the time." The pain pills another survivor received from her internist for pain "were just sitting on my medicine counter. I really didn't want to take any more medications because I'm leery now of trusting what is being given from my experience with HRT. So they remain there. They'll probably expire, and then I'll throw them out."

Not surprisingly, women were especially angry about advice to use some form of estrogen to relieve menopausal symptoms. A gynecologist's suggestion that Pat Garland try hormone replacement therapy horrified her. Convinced that therapy had contributed to her cancer, a second woman remained uncertain about trying a vaginal cream containing estrogen: "They're saying it's OK. That's what they said about hormone replacement therapy, so I don't know what to do. It's my life, and I don't want to mess it up again. I don't want any more cancer."

Prescriptions for antidepressants provoked other complaints. One was that doctors were too ready to view women's physical problems as psychological in nature. (In some cases, the doctors may have prescribed the medication "off label" for such conditions as pain or fatigue but failed to explain the reason.)[28] Another complaint was that doctors' primary motive was to rid themselves of difficult patients. One survivor charged, "Doctors are really easy to give you a prescription because they get you out of their hair." Another stated, "When I come in and I know that I've had all these different treatments, I expect [doctors] to take me seriously. I don't expect to be treated like a mental patient and thrown an antidepressant." A few women had tried antidepressants but then discontinued them when they exacerbated such postcancer symptoms as sexual disorders and memory loss.

Unable to learn about acceptable treatments from doctors, women again turned to other survivors. When Ida Jaffe's doctor refused to send her to a physical therapist for her lymphedema, she got a massage other women recommended. Another survivor received "a wealth of information" from members of her support group. "They have experience. They've been there. So, to me, that's the most accurate. I mean, you get the true feelings from the person. And you get tips from somebody. You say, 'What would you do for hot flashes?' And people say, 'Well, drink a lot of soy milk.' I mean, everybody has a little something to say."

The final criticism leveled against doctors challenged their claims of being compassionate. Assuming that physicians honored patients' humanity as well as their cancers, many women were dismayed to discover that their physicians seemed interested in symptoms only insofar as they signaled the possibility of a cancer recurrence. Just as Pat Garland's doctor would only "look for and give [her] cancer-related tests," so the back pain that forced Rose Jensen to abandon tennis was "not something the doctors give a lot of weight to." Rose concluded, "I don't think they'll take me seriously again until I have cancer. Otherwise it's 'Oh, you're fine. Goodbye.'" When asked how her oncologist responded to her various symptoms, a third woman answered, "She's just sort of like, 'You're better now,' so if she doesn't see anything wrong in the blood test and a few others things she looks at, then I seem to be doing OK. . . . I'm alive and things are going OK, so she just can take me off her list of worries." That comment illustrates what sociolinguist Elliot Mishler calls the conflict between the "World of Medicine" and the "Life World" of the patient.[29] Narrowing her gaze to biological phenomena that might indicate the cancer had returned, the doctor refused to acknowledge the entire scope of this woman's life.

Doctors also belittled problems that seemed unrelated to cancer. Leanne Thomas recalled, "One breast is larger than the other. And the doctor said, 'Well, people want big boobs.' And I said, 'Well, I don't. I never did.' I said, 'I don't want to have a breast job. Give me my small boobs back; that's all I want. I don't want any big boobs. I like the little ones.'" Three women complained about doctors who dismissed complaints of peripheral neuropathy as trivial. When one woman mentioned the pain and numbness in her fingers and toes to her physicians, "they just brushed it away." Asked whom she had contacted about the numbness in her feet, another woman responded, "I brought it up a couple of times with my oncologist. And his reaction, 'Well, you can walk, can't you?' So I thought, 'Forget that.'" The third woman reported, "The oncologist sent me to a neurologist because I have peripheral neuropathy and my left hand shakes, but that was another doctor that was troublesome to me. It was as if she was reprimanding me for even being concerned about it. She said, 'You've got breast cancer. You should be thankful you are alive.' It's just one of those times that was really upsetting to me."

Losing Trust

Because we neither observed medical encounters nor interviewed doctors, we had access to only one side of the interaction and thus cannot establish the validity of the women's retrospective accounts. The heightened emotions many women brought to each physician visit may well have led them to misinterpret or forget some of what was said to them. It also is likely that as studies of cancer's aftereffects multiply, more and more doctors will warn about the possibility of long-term symptoms before administering treatment, acknowledge the role of chemotherapy and radiation in their genesis, express concern about their impact on survivors' lives, and provide ample information about remedial resources. What the interviews do reveal, however, is that most survivors expected all doctors to respond knowledgeably and compassionately to posttreatment symptoms and that those expectations often were disappointed. The sense of disillusionment was especially intense when the doctors who had administered treatment dismissed any responsibility for the symptoms or displayed little empathy for the suffering they caused. In such cases, women began to wonder whether the doctors had been worthy of the respect invested in them.

We occasionally heard excuses for physicians: Medical knowledge accumulates so rapidly doctors cannot possibly keep up to date. "Do you know everything about what you do?" one survivor challenged us. "Nobody does." Insurance constraints prevent doctors from taking time to listen to patient concerns. And doctors must protect themselves emotionally by donning professional armor. A woman commented, "My oncologist is the one who's a little bit more cold toward things. I give her the excuse that she deals with people dying all the time." Another stated, "The oncologist just spouts, 'You need to do this and do that . . . ,' and when you sit down and try talking to them in person, they don't want to talk to you like a person. My experience and my friends' experience is that if you're an oncologist, you make sure you're not that emotionally involved with your patients because lots of them die."

But behaviors that could be explained still might undermine trust. Regardless of the reasons, one doctor remained "cold" and another refused to communicate with his patient as "a person." We asked all survivors how their symptoms affected their current relationships with members of their health care teams. Ida Jaffe, who previously had told us she had believed her doctors' "every word" at the beginning of treatment, answered, "I think I still have a good relationship, but I don't trust them as much as I trusted them at the outset of going into it." Jean Trawick "missed the honesty," a trait she previously had ascribed to her doctors. A third survivor commented, "I guess I'm a little bit jaded now in thinking that the medical profession doesn't know everything that it needs to know."

Many women also expressed their skepticism about physicians by relying on other survivors for medical information. And while listening to members of focus groups and support groups narrate their lives, the women drew parallels with themselves and reinforced their belief that survivors, not doctors, knew best.[30] Although Pat Garland's efforts to convince a friend and the Social Security Administration about the "reality" of her symptoms ultimately remained unsuccessful, she was able to gain the self-respect that came from retaining some distance from medical pronouncements and honoring the information she acquired experientially through her body.

A major report by the prestigious Institute of Medicine and National Research Council of the National Academies echoes many complaints we heard. Concluding that "the current system for delivering care to the growing number of cancer survivors is inadequate," services tend to be fragmented, and providers focus on "surveillance for recurrence and second cancers" rather than survivors' many other urgent concerns, the report calls for a multidisciplinary and coordinated system of follow-up care.[31] Such a system would have been an enormous boon to the survivors we interviewed, but it could never address the profound challenge they posed to the medical establishment. Even while continuing to look for physician validation and assistance, many women began to seek critical distance from medical authority. Following Foucault, one sociologist argues that "a pivotal arena of struggle in modern societies" is the "power . . . manifested in the ability of professionals to label, classify, and condemn, as well as in the capacity of clients to resist the imposition of such meanings."[32] Women became active participants in that struggle by giving credence to their own physical sensations in the face of physician skepticism and looking to other survivors as a source of medical knowledge.

As the next chapter shows, women who were discontented with doctors' ability to either diagnose their ills or ease their suffering also turned to alternative practitioners.

3

Remedying, Managing, and Making Do

LEANNE THOMAS NEVER expected doctors to resolve the many health problems she faced after breast cancer treatment. "I'm not one for taking a lot of medications," she told us. "I'm one for holistic. My family didn't go to doctors. They had things that you took that you didn't have to go to doctors for, natural things." Physicians were able to use her family history, which included the deaths of her mother and three aunts from breast cancer, to convince Leanne to undergo five months of chemotherapy and six weeks of radiation. Once her treatment was over, she relied on self-help and alternative remedies to address her ensuing difficulties, which included hot flashes, dental and vision problems, insomnia, memory loss, fatigue, and depression. Although she saw a dentist for her bleeding gums, the only physician she consulted about her other complaints was her oncologist, and she adamantly rejected his advice. His referral for psychotherapy was especially unwelcome. "I was like, 'Now I have to talk to a shrink? Am I crazy or something?'" Her memory of her experience when her mother was dying strengthened her resistance:

> The counselor was saying, "You're spending all this time with your mother. You go there at lunch time and go there after work and stay with her." I said, "That's my mother, that's the only mother that I have." She said, "You need to get a life." And I say, "*You* need to get a life. That's my life right there, that's my mother."
>
> That's why, when they said to see a psychiatrist, I was like, "Oh my goodness, what are they going to say? What do they know?" It took me a while, but I was desperate. It's not like I was going to

commit suicide or anything, but I was crying, laying in bed, and feeling sorry, and I was trying to eat and I wasn't getting anything down. The only thing I would do—I knew that the bills were due. I didn't want things to get cut off. I'd go out and pay those. Then I'd come back home and say, "OK, you finished that so you can stay in bed now." And I would do that.

As Leanne's depression deepened, she finally agreed to seek therapy:

I found myself opening up and talking, and it felt good. And I started doing things and making gestures and everything. It helped me—it did—and it felt good. She saw me one day when I came in, and I was all dressed and I had my hair done. She goes, "You look so nice." And I said, "Yes, I decided to put something else on today." I was putting on my little stuff and getting out there. Before I'd just say, "I'm just going to the doctor. Put on my sweats." This time I said, "I'll do this and that." And she says, "Oh, you're coming out. You're doing good." And I said, "Thank you, I feel good." And she says, "You look good." And we were just talking. That helped, and that's what I needed.

Leanne tried to resolve other symptoms without professional assistance. By adding vitamins, fruits, and vegetables to her diet, she had begun to regain her strength. Yoga relieved some of her stress. For those symptoms that could not be alleviated, she tried to find other coping methods. For example, putting her keys in a certain place at home helped to compensate for her memory lapses. She also took frequent naps to accommodate her fatigue:

I just have to take time to do things now, and I just have to rest. I just can't be rushing around doing this and doing that. I have to follow my body. When my body said it's tired, it's tired. And people might say, "Every time I call you, you're in bed." I just say, "You know what, I'm resting. I have to do this, and I'm doing it. You can say whatever you want to say. I don't care." I said, "That's it. I'm going through something, and I don't know how long I will be going through it. But I'm going to obey my body."

Other help came from religion: "I pray; I ask the Lord for guidance and to show me the way, and I let go. Not that I wasn't praying before; I always prayed. But I'm listening now. I think I'm at another point in my life where I can hear. I say, 'You know what's right for me to do and how to handle these situations.' So I've become more involved in the church." To strengthen her commitment, she joined a bible study group and began to teach at the Sunday school. And she concluded she survived for a reason: "I'm asking the Lord, 'What is my purpose here? Is there something that you want me to do because I made it through here?'"

Although Leanne had an exceptionally strong motivation to look beyond the medical community for help with her postcancer symptoms, she was not alone in doing so. The search for remedies takes many survivors not only to oncologists, radiologists, and other medical doctors but also to psychologists, physical therapists, and a wide variety of alternative practitioners; in addition, women draw heavily on a vast array of self-care measures. Experimenting with treatment options they previously spurned, some women, like Leanne, find their lives opening in positive ways. But many therapies also impose significant costs, especially of time and money. Although some forms of alternative care and self-help seek to boost the immune system, reassert control, or address the acute side effects of treatment and the sequelae of surgery, many others serve as ways to cope with the broad array of health problems medical studies have only recently begun to document.

Alternative Health Care

Alternative medicine typically is defined as any therapy not commonly taught in medical school or practiced in hospitals. According to a widely cited study by David M. Eisenberg and his colleagues, the use of such health care is both extensive and rapidly growing in the United States. In 1997, 43 percent of Americans reported using some form of alternative medicine during the past year, up from 34 percent in 1990.[1] As table 3.1 demonstrates, rates of use for several alternative therapies among the survivors in our study were extremely high. The figures can be explained in various ways. Although users of alternative medicine are less likely than others to be African American, they are more likely to be women

TABLE 3.1

USE OF ALTERNATIVE THERAPIES

Therapy	Abel/Subramanian Sample*	Eisenberg et al. Sample**
Herbal medicine	38%	12.1%
Massage	49%	11.1%
Chiropractic	38%	11.0%
Homeopathy	19%	3.4%
Hypnosis	17%	1.2%
Biofeedback	24%	1.0%
Acupuncture	28%	1.0%
Energy healing	16%	3.8%

* "Use" refers to use of alternative therapies at any time to address post-breast-cancer symptoms.
** "Use" refers to use within the past twelve months in 1997. Source: David M. Eisenberg et al., "Trends in Alternative Medicine Use in the United States, 1990–1997: Results of a Follow-Up National Survey," JAMA, v. 280, no. 18 (November 11, 1998): 1569–1574.

and to have recently undergone a transformative experience.[2] Moreover, the women we interviewed suffered from some of the chronic conditions most frequently treated with alternative medicine (pain, fatigue, and anxiety).[3] Many alternative therapies claim not just to provide symptom relief but also to boost the immune system, a crucial concern for all cancer survivors.[4] And cancer patients often are bombarded with information about alternative care, both during and after treatment.

Like Leanne, a few women described themselves as having used alternative care long before cancer struck. "I'm from Jamaica," one survivor stated. "The way I was brought up is about a lot of natural and holistic eating. I was born on a farm in the country. My grandmother knew nothing but herbs, and she brought me up that way, and I kept that cultural state with me." Although Tessa McKnight was the only one in her family to use nontraditional treatment, she had long been committed to it. "It may sound kind of funny," she began, "but I see someone who's a healer, and I've been working with him since I was first diagnosed. . . . I wasn't even gonna do chemo. I was gonna go and try and do some alternative thing in Mexico. I believe in that, because I believe that if you can raise the immune system really high, then it can fight what's going on in the body. But I think that my cancer was really aggressive and fast growing. My alternative doctor, who I went to get help on deciding what to do alternatively, just was like, 'You gotta start chemo like yesterday.' So my natural propensity is to go towards alternative stuff." The holistic beliefs underlying alternative medicine motivated another survivor: "I've always felt that it's a body-mind-spirit and just not the body, and you have to have an inner spirit. I don't think it's God. It can be you. So I've always been in that space that I'm open to complementary medicine."[5]

More commonly, dissatisfaction with conventional medicine spurred the use of alternative treatments.[6] One woman, for example, saw herself "becoming totally antimedication." "Grant you," she continued, "when you are going through cancer you do whatever is extreme so you can get through it. But once you're through it you don't want to add to the problems, because you see the radiation has done some damage and the chemotherapy has done some damage. So from that point on you want to build up rather than cause new problems."

Jean Trawick coupled her discussion of her alternative medicine experience with a diatribe against the health care she had received since her diagnosis. A doctor's daughter, she "grew up in a household where if you mentioned the word 'osteopath,' [her] father had a fit." Anger at the way doctors treated her, however, put Jean "on the road to look for other things." By the time we spoke with her, she had tried biofeedback, acupuncture, herbology, reflexology, and chiropractic. Her primary provider was a nurse practitioner trained in both Western and alternative medicine.

Women who overcame long-term skepticism of alternative remedies often were pleasantly surprised. Before exploring meditation, one survivor had always thought she could not "really sit in a room and go 'ummmm.'" "But it's different now. I realize it helps me kind of hold back and get in touch with my body. And I realized the strength of those kinds of things." Another convert to meditation had previously dismissed it as "too hippylike." "It didn't seem like it was more until I tried it," she commented. But not all forms of care received equally good reports. Massage was too "intimate" to some, biofeedback too much like "Frankenstein," and acupuncture too similar to "crucifixion."

Women who avoided alternative medicine entirely tended to divide into two groups. Some were as adamantly opposed to nontraditional therapies as Leanne was to conventional medicine. When we began to list various treatments, a woman interrupted us, saying, "I'm not into that. I just take medication. I strictly want a pill." Asked if she had any plans to try different therapies, another survivor responded, "No. No, I don't. I'm going to stick to what they're telling me. I'm not going through that alternative medicine or running down to Mexico and letting people in Mexico do anything to me. No, I'm going to stay right here and do what they tell me using conventional medicine."

Others endorsed alternative treatments in principle but balked at the time or money involved. One remarked, "I think an effect of having had cancer and having had treatments and having to go for follow-up blood tests—and I go for follow-up breast exams—is I don't want to see any more doctors. I'm conscientious about seeing the doctors that I need to see, but electively, whereas before this I might have been willing to see an acupuncturist twice a week. Now I'd rather just deal with the pain." Visits to alternative practitioners were not an option for many women with full-time jobs or onerous responsibilities at home. A lawyer remarked, "I've been meaning to try acupuncture if I ever could find time out of this office." Because few health insurance plans cover nontraditional therapies, most patients pay out of pocket.[7] Some women found the cost prohibitive. "Massages really help," one told us, "but the lady that I went to is sixty dollars an hour, and that is out of my range right now." Pat Garland would like to try herbs, but "sixty dollars and eighty dollars a bottle for a three-day supply I can't afford."

There were other problems as well. Surrounded by a vast array of possible treatments, women had few ways to discover which would work best for them. No reputable guides existed about quality. And many women worried about the fragmentation of care. Studies conclude that most people view alternative therapies as a complement to, rather than a substitute for, mainstream medicine.[8] We can assume that cancer survivors would be especially reluctant to reject traditional health care. Even women who explained their use of alternative medicine by pointing to the deficiencies of conventional care hoped their doctors would be able to coordinate the two modalities. Most physicians, however, were unable to do so. Rose Jensen said,

I would like to have a doctor that knew enough about supplements so that I could have a really thoughtful discussion about what would be beneficial or if I'm blowing my money on alpha-lipic acid or whether it's helping me. Because if you go to an alternative doctor, they're going to say, "Of course it's gonna help you." If you go to a traditional Western doctor, they'll say, "There's no reason why it should help you." So it would be nice to have a medical professional who either worked together or who had a wider span of knowledge, but at the moment it seems like you have to go to a discrete person for everything. There's no agreement.

Greta Shaw encountered greater hostility: "I do like alternative and a little bit more holistic kinds of things, but I wish there was more of a connection with the regular MD. It really creates a problem for me when I go to the doctor, to my internist or oncologist, and I'll mention something about I went to see an alternative or holistic doctor and it's just friction. They just don't believe that they work together that well. Especially my internist, she's young, and she's very, very bright, and she's very narrow-minded." Even doctors who embraced the idea of alternative medicine knew little about it. When Tessa McKnight gave her oncologist a list of the homeopathic remedies and herbal supplements her healer had prescribed, he "was just great; he was all into it." But he also assumed Tessa was "doing" her "homework," investigating the possibility of any adverse interactions on her own.

Psychological and Physical Therapies

One of the sharpest differences between the African American and white women we interviewed was their attitudes toward psychotherapy. For the white women, discussing emotional problems with a therapist seemed almost routine. Many had consulted therapists long before receiving cancer diagnoses and assumed they would do so again during future periods of heightened stress. Most of the black women, by contrast, had associated psychotherapy with mental illness. One recalled that when persistent insomnia finally convinced her to agree to see a psychologist, other African American women tried to dissuade her. "It just got to the point where I needed to talk to somebody other than my pastor. But when I did tell some of the girls in the breast cancer support group that I was going, they said, 'You ain't crazy. You don't need to go to do that.'" Like Leanne Thomas, Annie Briggs eventually became an enthusiast:

> My oncologist from Kaiser Permanente suggested that I see a shrink. In terms of African Americans, that's not something we do. We think that is a Caucasian thing, when they're ready to close on their half-million-dollar home. But I beg to differ. It has been such an enhancement for me to be able to vent openly to someone that I don't know personally. ... I could sit down and vent to my shrink for half an hour, and it's the most refreshing thing for me. I had a lot of negative thoughts about seeing shrinks, and it has been the best thing that could have happened to me. And I encourage all African American women—I say African American women because I am an African American and we have this tunnel vision about sitting down and discussing our problems—unless you try something, you don't know what it feels like.

Unlike alternative medicine and psychotherapy, physical therapy rarely aroused intense emotions. Lymphedema sufferers were especially likely to visit physical therapists, who employ massage, wrap affected limbs in special bandages, and teach simple exercises.[9] Many women expressed gratitude when swelling and pain diminished and arms moved more freely. Two African American women, however, charged that racial discrimination affected their treatment. One noted that the compression sleeves provided by her therapist matched the skin color of whites and looked ridiculous on her arm. Ida Jaffe asserted that her oncologist referred only his white patients to physical therapists; because she had to pay out of pocket, she could afford only minimal care.

Self-Help

Although researchers define self-help in a multitude of ways, most agree that it constitutes the bulk of care people receive, especially for chronic conditions. Here we include as self-care any actions survivors take without medical supervision, either to address their symptoms or reassert control over their lives.

Women with memory loss used brain exercises to restore function. One explained why she returned to school: "I think the more I push myself, the more I will gain back. I have heard that people do get brain function back, and there's a lot of research that in fact brain cells do regenerate, or their pathways. What's it called? Neurosynapse does develop, and that's what I'm going on." Crossword puzzles helped another woman keep her "cognitive outlook sharp." A third woman realized that the high school workbooks she bought for her nephew might help her as well: "I do a lot of the math and the word problems. I find if I keep my mind moving and learning, then it's getting better." A fourth took up an elaborate form of embroidery: "It's embroidery that looks like painting, but it's silk; it's very fine. It's an artistic expression, but it's also something that's very detailed and very focused. I think that's a way to mentally keep alert."

Other strategies sought to manage symptoms rather than alleviate them. When fatigue was a problem, women employed various forms of energy conservation. Like Leanne, a nurse monitored herself throughout the day: "I pace myself. I never did that before. I always did everything until I dropped. I pay more attention. I have to. If I get tired, I have to lie down." An accountant learned from a friend with chronic fatigue symptoms: "Thank God I'm not in that condition, but she's given me a lot of little tips. Like I have more meals, more small meals, putting your head down on your desk for ten minutes. Things like that." Linguistic changes helped another survivor slow down: "I've taken the action words from my vocabulary. In other words, 'I've gotta rush over here,' 'Let me hurry and do that.'" An educational consultant reduced her expectations for herself on the job:

> My work involves a lot of travel. I used to get up at three in the morning to get to El Centro and then drive home at the end of the day. So that was eight hours of driving and eight hours of working. I do not do that to myself anymore. I go the day before, I get a hotel room, and if we work until five, I don't drive home at the end of the day tired. I get a hotel room, and I drive home leisurely the next morning. And when I go on my consulting, I never fly in anymore

and take the cab to work. I tell them, "If you will not put me up the night before and the night after, I'm not coming." Now frankly, I should have done it a long time ago!

Women also found ways to work within cognitive limitations. Just as Leanne Thomas left her keys in a certain place at home, so Ida Jaffe parked in the same spot each time she went to the mall. Greta Shaw tried to "de-clutter" her house, explaining, "If I really don't have a lot of stuff around me, if I set something down, then hopefully it will jump out." Several women wrote notes to themselves or asked others to convey information in writing. One said, "I have post-its all over my refrigerator, all over my mirror, and everywhere. And I told my daughter, 'You know, you're very special to me. I want to always be a part of your life, but I don't remember so well. So if there's something important to you, you have to tell me three or four times or give it to me in a note.'" Other women scrupulously followed the detailed plans they made in advance for each day.

Impression management also consumed women's attention. In a classic study, sociologist Erving Goffman argues that stigmatized individuals try to "pass" by hiding their "spoiled identities" as far as possible.[10] Concealment begins early in the breast cancer career. Attitudes have changed greatly since the early twentieth century, when breast cancer was so stigmatized that women hesitated to disclose their diagnosis, occasionally even to intimates.[11] But if women rarely still hide disease labels, many do seek to camouflage the most conspicuous consequences. The most dramatic form, of course, is reconstructive surgery, far from a self-help measure. Two forms, however, fall under the rubric of self-help: wigs and cosmetics to conceal the acute effects of chemotherapy, and prostheses to hide the results of mastectomies. Both have received feminist criticism. Poet Audre Lorde railed against the widespread insistence that she wear a prosthesis after her mastectomy. A Reach to Recovery volunteer who visited Lorde after her mastectomy "outraged and insulted" her by offering an inset for her bra. When a nurse castigated Lorde's failure to wear a prosthesis to a follow-up appointment, Lorde felt she had received an "assault on my right to define and to claim my own body."[12] Other feminist complaints target the "Look Good, Feel Good" programs sponsored jointly by the American Cancer Society and charitable organizations supported by cosmetic manufacturers and held in hospitals for women undergoing chemotherapy. As Sharon Batt writes, "The intense promotion of prostheses and cosmetics, coupled with the coercive tactics used on those who eschew them, signal that these accessories are not really meant for our benefit."[13]

Women in our study commented less on the oppressive nature of various forms of concealment than on their cost. Wigs, makeup, and prostheses both diminished the sympathy available to women and left them vulnerable to exposure. Pat Garland spoke to the first issue: "It was my nature to put on my eyebrows, and it was my nature to put a little lipstick on. And I would go to the church, and the minister—I'm [feeling like] I'm dying here—and he's like, 'But you look so good!' And I'm like, 'Could you give me a hug? Because I think I'm going to be in a box real soon.' But I'll look real good!" Doctors and nurses also were convinced she was as well as she appeared: "You go in, and you tell them you're hurting and this is bothering you. But I'm not going to come to the hospital in my nightgown." A television producer emphasized the precariousness of disguise. One of the few women who refused to disclose her diagnosis at work, she explained, "Entertainment is not a giving or kindly profession, and if you're damaged goods, you're gone—particularly if you are aging damaged goods. And since I was already in my forties, I felt it very important to keep this a secret." As a result, she donned a wig as soon as she experienced hair loss. But her job "involved being on the road and often sharing a room with someone, so it was physically awkward." Although she removed her wig only at night under the cover of darkness, she constantly worried that she would unwittingly betray her "secret."

Prostheses provoked similar problems. One survivor noted that her "normal" appearance encouraged friends to assume her troubles were over and she could now "get on" with her life. One incident served as an example: "I was with a group of ladies. They had provided a masseuse, and I refused to have the massage because after having the mastectomy I'm shy in terms of my body. And they kept pressing, and they knew that I had gone through the surgery and different things like that. And one of the girlfriends there made the comment, 'But you just seem so normal.' And so I had to explain to her." The producer resorted to a prosthesis after ten years of surgeries failed to control the infections from a breast implant. She again stressed the dangers of exposure: "The prosthesis kept falling out, which was awfully embarrassing, usually on the tennis court, occasionally during an interview. So, yeah, there was anxiety over that."

Memory loss is another symptom women struggled to camouflage. When one survivor forgot words in a conversation, for example, she "changed the subject, played it off as something else." Because the consequences of disclosing cognitive impairments at work could be especially severe, even women who revealed their problems at home took special care to conceal them on the job. One woman expressed gratitude toward a partner who "covered" for her. Fund-raiser Nina Worth relied on a subordinate: "I was forever asking my assistant, 'OK, what's the word that means, you know, this, this, and this?' and trying to describe to her so she could come up with the word for me." Others referred to themselves as "bluffing" or "faking." As a subordinate, a legal secretary was expected to serve as her boss's memory: "He would say, 'Remember that document that we did last week?' And I would say, 'No, I don't remember. But then why would I remember? It's not my document.' Or I would say, 'I think I remember. Give me a few more clues. Well, let me look,' and sort of try and fake it and hope that I would come up with the right thing. It was scary."

Concealment also took more subtle forms. When a professor lost her train of thought in the middle of a lecture, she thought "really fast" to ensure that the lapse was not "grossly noticeable" to her students. An elementary school teacher extended her work week. When asked whether her cognitive dysfunction affected her ability to do her job, she replied, "My performance, absolutely not. Not once I was over the chemo. It's made it harder for me to do it, but from the standpoint of my administrators they should not have noticed anything other than I worked a lot longer hours and I have to organize myself a lot more so I don't forget to do things. I mean everything has to be just so. I have to plan the day before because it has to be laid out."

Like other forms of "passing," however, the concealment of memory loss often took a toll. The schoolteacher's long hours cut into her leisure time, just when her need for relaxation had increased. Thinking "really fast" on her feet often exhausted the professor's last energy reserves. And as a legal secretary discovered, faking could be "scary" because it carried the risk of exposure.

Humor also helped to preserve a public image. Jokes about "chemo-brain" filled the interviews, implying that losing track of conversations and forgetting words were simply humorous and trivial lapses rather than indications of serious problems. Asked what strategies she used to address her memory loss, one women answered, "I just kind of go with it and make a joke of it, because it is kind of funny." But humor was rarely an adequate solution. "I laugh with my friends about Alzheimer's. I say maybe some of that is settling in, in terms of this disease," Annie Briggs remarked and then acknowledged, "but it is very depressing to forget little minute things that you should remember." Greta Shaw said, "I always try to make some kind of fun of [my memory loss], but you know, it really does hurt." A third woman commented, "The cognitive thing—I joke about it, but it really just worries me."

Asserting Control

It is unsurprising that talk about the need to rebuild a sense of control pervaded the interviews. One of the most serious psychological results of trauma is a sense of profound helplessness.[14] Chronic-disease sufferers also frequently lament their inability to regulate their lives.[15] And cancer frequently is depicted as cells that are spinning out of control. The women in this study sought to regain control in diverse ways. One changed her hair style:

> I lost my hair as a result of the chemotherapy, and I had very thick and full hair. After I had the chemotherapy, it was really important for me to grow it back and to look the way I have looked before. I really needed that. And then I really felt like I wanted some change. So I started to cut my hair. But an element also for me in cutting my hair was that I wanted to be able to do it electively, to have a choice in the matter, and also for my kids to see me in short hair and associate it with my being healthy and not my having been ill. That was very deliberate.

For another survivor, alternative medicine represented an assertion of autonomy: "There's the breast cancer—one of the terrible things is that you are no longer in control of your life. You are being controlled, and for someone who'd always been fairly successful and fairly in charge, that was very difficult. So, by attempting other therapies, I think to some extent I was trying to regain some kind of control over my life."

Above all, women restored a sense of mastery by making lifestyle changes. As health writer Gina Kolata notes, "America's popular and commercial cultures promote the idea of an inexhaustible capacity for self-rejuvenation and self-repair."[16] Ignoring the effects of pollution, genetics, and adverse life circumstances, magazine and newspaper articles proclaim it is never too late to restore health through proper eating and regular exercise. Although the survivors we interviewed had failed to return to their precancer selves, they shared the reigning assumption that people can prevent future disease by asserting careful control over their bodies. When we asked the women what they had done to address their symptoms, many answered by telling us how they had changed their lives to ensure optimal health. Emphasizing the power of individual choice and personal responsibility, the women simultaneously increased their sense of efficacy and berated themselves for past behavior. One said, "Why did I get breast cancer? What caused me? What do I need to do differently so that I don't get it again? Even if I had no symptoms after all the treatment, I still would be facing the fact that I had breast cancer. I need to do something different." Ida Jaffe's response was similar:

> For me, I exercise a lot. I start off the morning with a three-mile walk. I walk about three miles each morning. I'm on the track at about 5:30 in the morning. So I exercise. I've changed my diet. I've lost about twenty-five pounds since the onset of cancer. I eat more fruits and vegetables. I drink a lot of water. Before cancer I was a junk-food junkie—hamburgers, potato chips, sodas, the whole bit. . . . I have to realize that I played a part in my own health and where I was in my health. I was not eating properly, taking care of my body properly, and things like that. Now I'm taking an active part, so I feel I'm more in charge.

Making Do

What about "acceptance," the stage chronic-disease sufferers are enjoined to reach? A catch phrase cancer survivors frequently encounter is the "new normal." Rather than struggling against all odds to return to the precancer status quo, they are urged to make peace with their limitations. Attempts to manage symptoms suggest some measure of acceptance. So do comments such as the following:

> My symptoms are part of my life. It's not like I have a cold and it's going away. The lymphedema is not going away; it's permanent. The tugging from the implant is permanent. The chemobrain is obviously permanent. So I don't see them as symptoms anymore; I see them as, "this is how my life is now." It sucks; it will always suck. But if I spend all of my time thinking about how rotten it is, I'm not going to have any life. So you just kind of move on.

> My symptoms are not something that I really talk about anymore. I just live with them. I've just accepted that this is what it is and try to address them as much as I can and resolve them to the point that I can and then go on. So it's not an ongoing thing. The symptoms are ongoing, but my need to address them isn't.

Counting their blessings helped some women come to terms with their symptoms. Over and over these survivors emphasized that the cancer had not spread, the treatment had been relatively easy, they had escaped the most serious side effects, and they remained in remission.

Nevertheless, acceptance was more often a goal than an achievement for the women in our study. (A major reason may have been the timing of the interviews, in some cases just a year after the end of treatment.) "I know there's a 'new normal' for me someplace," one woman said, "but I'm still running to try to get back to who I was." Contradictory tenses in self-descriptions also betrayed a lack of acquiescence in the "new normal." For example, a survivor said first, "I've always been a high-energy, energetic person," then "I don't have the energy I had before," and finally both things at once, "I often have no energy to do things I want to do. See, I am a very active person." In a similar vein, Annie Briggs said, "I can do two things out of one day, and I'm exhausted; I am totally exhausted. I am a very vibrant person."

Moreover, several women refused to abandon a quest for solutions that had begun to seem increasingly futile. One, for example, continued to take Aleve despite its failure to lessen her pain "because it's really frustrating to feel like there is nothing you can do. I think it's to avoid the hopelessness times." After six years of consulting an "enormous" number of both traditional doctors and alternative practitioners for her mouth problem, Greta Shaw declared herself "burned out." Nine months before we interviewed her she had announced her intention to give up. But that meant reconciling herself to a painful condition that frequently disrupted her life. Having recently heard of a woman in Westlake who possibly might have the answer, Greta wondered if perhaps she should seek one more consultation. And always in the back of her mind was the possibility of traveling to the Mayo Clinic to see the doctor who had identified the disorder that had plagued her for so long.

Costs and Benefits

Facing a broad array of poorly understood physical health problems, the breast cancer survivors in our study tried one remedy after another. Alternative health care, physical therapy, and psychotherapy provided relief for certain symptoms but consumed time and money the women could ill afford. To the extent that self-help measures involved simplifying life, they often seemed long overdue. After imposing strict boundaries on her work day, one woman realized she should have done so "a long time ago." Greta Shaw removed the household clutter that had annoyed her for years. Other forms of self-care had costs as well as benefits. Although lifestyle changes provided a sense of control and possibly improved health status, strict adherence to the philosophy of personal responsibility reinforced women's tendency to blame themselves for developing cancer. The concealment that allowed survivors to "pass" in public reduced the amount of sympathy they received and placed them at risk of exposure. Humor helped cover humiliating memory lapses but could not restore personal esteem, eliminate the frustrations of diminished cognition, or stave off fears of a worsening condition.

4

"Like Talking to a Wall"

THREE AFRICAN AMERICAN women met during a focus group to discuss the ways breast cancer affects social relationships both during and after therapy. Ida Jaffe began:

My family was very supportive in helping me. My husband was very supportive, and I have two daughters, and they were just right there for me. But I did have an experience with a so-called friend. I'll say a so-called friend because she was there through all of the initial part of the treatment, right at the beginning and everything. Then after all the chemo and radiation and everything was over, and I was still bald, she said, "Why don't you wear a wig?" And I said, "Because I really don't care to wear a wig. It's just not my thing. I'm bald headed, just bald headed. Accept me like I am." And she said, "You need to get back into life. Let's get back to shopping." And I said, "You know, I just can't really do it at this time. I'm not feeling like it." She said, "You know what? You need to get over this. You're just carrying this cancer thing a little bit too far." And I thought, "Oh really, that's how you feel?" And she says, "Yeah, you know," she says, "it's over. You're treated, you're healed. Get on with life!"

And my family, I would tell them things up to a point. After a while you burn people out. They're burned out on your being tired, and the fears that you have. So if you ask me, then I'll tell you. But if you don't ask me, I really don't need to tell you. This thing, this cancer, you're in it on your own. I mean, yes, everybody's concerned about you, and everybody wants the best for you, but it's you. You're alone.

The next speaker was Marsha Dixler:

When I was diagnosed, I had been divorced for several years and my daughter, I guess she was fourteen. And I had been dating a guy for several years. He couldn't deal with it. He related my breast cancer to a root canal. A root canal! But that's a man. At first that was real, real hurtful. At the time I need you the most, and we've been together for years. You of all people know me better than anybody, and now you can't deal with it. And then I found out that he had moved some other lady in with him, like in a matter of three or four months after we broke up.

But then I have a very supportive family. My sister loves me unconditionally. Two brothers, if I would ever hear them say no to me, that's when I'll probably faint. I mean never in my life have I ever called them and said anything, and they said no. Every single surgery that I had—my sister lives in Little Rock—every single surgery she came out here. And I even know on a couple of occasions she had had to have some type of surgery herself; she had them give her a local so she could come out here and be with me, because she knew I would have been by myself. And then she didn't tell me that. She did that because I would have been mad. But to find out something like that, to know you have a sister that will go under a knife locally just to come and be with you, then all the stuff with that guy, it wasn't real anyway.

Pat Garland continued the discussion:

My family was a little bit different from you guys'. We're a very small family. First of all, my mother only had four children. And my mother died from breast cancer. So when I was diagnosed at forty something, my two sisters could not deal with it. They just totally panicked. My daughter was in her twenties. She panicked. She told me every time she saw me her breasts would hurt. My son, he really didn't take it too well, because everybody in my family saw death. One sister came from Texas; her and her husband, they had prepared to give up their home to nurse me until I died. So they all remembered my mother's experience. They forgot that my mother lived fifteen years after being diagnosed with breast cancer. She eventually died of stomach cancer. So everybody was scared, but everybody was willing to make the sacrifices that were needed to take care of me.

And my girlfriend, she took me to chemotherapy every time. She cooked for me, she cleaned for me, she took care of me. She was there in the morning with fruit, watermelon, all kinds of stuff for me to eat, after I got sick. So that's how I made it through.

But I have to keep what's going on with me now to myself. There's not a lot of people I can tell. Even the friend that took me to chemotherapy. We go to the Pomona fair together, and she's like, "You need to lose some weight because you can't walk." You were there for me during chemotherapy, but now she didn't understand that I need the little go-cart to go around the Pomona fairgrounds. I could not keep up. So these are the kinds of friends that I have that are close to me, that know me by name, and take care of me. They will if I was sick, sick, sick, sick. But to understand that there's a troubled life after the original diagnosis, they don't get it. They do not get it, and I can say it with you women. I wouldn't say it to them. They're not there for me. The more you tell the outside world your limitations, the more they tell you no. The more they tell you, "You can do it." Everybody calls me when somebody in their lives have cancer. And I work with them until whatever. My daughter-in-law just called me because she's got some thirty-year-old that's dying from testicular cancer. And she was like, "Well, Mom, he's denying, he won't get his affairs in order. Do you think you could talk to his wife?" Yeah, I can talk to her and help her understand his process because he doesn't have long to go, so he really needs to get his things in order. But I would wish that sometimes they would call me and remember that I had cancer and it had an effect on me.

"Weeding People Out"

According to most of the women in our study, the responses of family members, close friends, and lovers to the difficulties experienced during treatment differed dramatically. Some (like Marsha's boyfriend) behaved abominably; the rest (including Marsha's sister) acted magnificently. Although there may indeed have been no middle ground, it also is possible that the women magnified both negative and supportive responses. "In the aftermath of traumatic life events," one psychiatrist explains, "survivors are highly vulnerable. Their sense of self has been shattered. That sense can be rebuilt only as it was built initially, in connection with others."[1] Thus, women undergoing brutal treatments while still reeling from breast cancer diagnoses may be exquisitely sensitive to the people around them. Every slight becomes a grievous betrayal, every caring response a sign of both the meaningfulness of life and the possible renewal of trust.

Women who had received extensive breast surgery needed proof of their attractiveness and desirability from sexual partners. One woman's husband helped to counter her sense of defilement: "When I couldn't look at myself and call myself beautiful, he was able to do that." Because a second woman's marriage was troubled, she had little reason to believe her husband would offer the comfort she sought. Nevertheless, his response wounded her deeply: "I don't think he's ever looked at my breast since it was cut up. If he has, he must have peeked when I wasn't looking. And I'm sensitive to that. I'm sensitive that either he doesn't want to see or he's repulsed by it." Another possibility, that perhaps he chose not to look out of concern for her modesty or feelings, did not occur to her.

Many survivors severed contact with friends who had disappointed. Thus, Jean Trawick explained why she lost touch with a high school classmate: "I said, 'Could you help me out?' And she said, 'Well, if you get stuck with groceries, call me, and I won't charge you very much.' So I am no longer in communication with her." Marge Barlow told us, "The people who could not be responsive to me when I was sick, I stopped talking to them altogether. They said, 'Oh, it's just too upsetting for me to see you,' and I thought, 'Well, you need to put your feelings aside at this point.' So if they couldn't, I dropped them." Another woman used a horticultural metaphor to underscore the need to cull relationships:

> It's interesting when you have breast cancer because you find out who are the people that are really your friends. And it's kind of a process of weeding people out. Pay attention to people who are really generous and kind and good—those are the friendships to be cultivated. It's very interesting. I had two friends from high school who were really good friends; we would get together socially, and to me it was amazing. When I was diagnosed with breast cancer in November, I never saw them ever, and finally in February we went out to dinner, and they must have asked me a few questions, and it was kind of like, "Move on to what's more interesting." That was just so hurtful. At that moment, I just thought, "These are the people you need to weed out of your life."

But we also heard many examples of intimates and friends who greatly exceeded expectations. One survivor cried when she talked about her husband: "His mom had cancer, and she died before he and I met, and I was so afraid he would leave me. But he didn't at all! No, he was just the opposite. He wouldn't leave! I'm OK, leave me alone. Just the love that he has, it's just incredible." Because American society exalts the value of self-sufficiency, sick people often hesitate to ask for help.[2] By reframing dependency, Tessa McKnight was able to find unanticipated pleasure in the care her friends bestowed:

> At first when I went to chemo treatments, they said, "Bring somebody with you because you don't know how you're going to feel." They didn't particularly want you driving home alone afterwards. And I kept thinking, "I don't want to burden any of my friends with that." But one of the nurses in my oncologist's office, I told her that. I said, "I just don't want to burden my friends with having to go through this." And she said, "Let me tell you something. You're doing them a favor by asking them, because you make them feel important and wanted." So I had eight treatments, and I got eight

friends. We had them lined up. And it turned out afterwards I felt really good. They gave you enough drugs so that you're in "lala land." So we either went shopping or out to lunch. We had a lovely day. So when she told me this, and I saw the reaction, I knew it wasn't a burden to them.

Support also occasionally came from unexpected sources. When a woman in a clerical job took five months of leave without pay to undergo treatment, her colleagues surprised her by donating their vacation time. Tessa received help from strangers:

> I called a lot of the credit card people that I owed money to, and they wanted money now. And I'd call them and I told my story: "I have breast cancer. I'm going through chemo. I don't have money. I want to pay you, but I can't pay you the whole thing. Can I do a settlement with you?" So I actually had a lot of conversations with different people and was able to settle accounts. I only had to pay like 50 percent of what I owed them. And you know, that was a thing I learned from this whole thing. There's people out there, it's not just big corporations and stuff. And if you just start talking to people, tell them what your situation is, then they can always bend rules or whatever. So that was good.

Marge Barlow recalled,

> My neighbor, one day I heard a lawn mower, and he was just over mowing my lawn. And he said, "Oh, I'll just take care of your yard until you're better." I also had some women come up to me when I was sick. I shaved my head bald because I thought that would be really interesting. And I would be sitting somewhere having lunch like at a counter, and a woman with that hair, that posttreatment hair growing in, would sit next to me and she would say, "Are you in treatment?" like out of the blue. . . . I kind of liked that. It made me feel good to see people that were recovered. Their hair was back, and they were reaching out to me in a really nice way.

Caregiving Responsibilities

Rather than receiving support, some patients and survivors had to provide it themselves. Despite the enormous changes the feminist movement has wrought in the distribution of domestic labor, women still do the great bulk of child rearing and caring for sick family members.[3] A breast cancer diagnosis failed to exempt one woman from those obligations: "At the time when I was in my treatment I had two little babies at home, and my mother was dying of breast cancer in my house. This was like amazing." Family responsibilities even determined her choice of therapy. When doctors recommended a stem-cell transplant, she refused to "contemplate" such a procedure, assuming her children and mother could not tolerate her absence during the long hospital stay required.

Although some women were enraged when friends and family invoked their own fears as an excuse for withholding support, others had tried to shield the people around them from the trauma of diagnosis and treatment.[4] A nurse explained why she was "the perfect patient—never complaining, always smiling," when she received chemotherapy: "My friends were work friends. We all worked oncology, and I had chosen to be treated at the place where I worked. . . . I wasn't going to sit around there and go, 'Damn, this sucks! God, can't you guys do anything better than this?!'"

Needless to say, women were especially solicitous of children.[5] "I just had to stay strong," recalled a single mother of two school-age children. "I never broke down around them. That was the toughest part because I always had a smile. I'd say I was doing well, when I wasn't feeling well." Rose Jensen's daughters were four and eight at the time of her diagnosis:

> They knew that I had cancer. They knew what was happening. They knew that the chemotherapy was making me ill, and that's why my hair fell out and that's why I didn't have energy. What I did was that I told them that the medicines I was taking that were making me sick were going to make me well. And my eight-year-old was told in class that just because I was taking chemotherapy didn't mean that I would live, that I could still die. And she came home from school very angry

that I hadn't said that, that I had made it seem that once this was over, it was over. And I said, "Well, anybody can die at any time, but hopefully this will keep me alive for a long time." But she still felt very angry. My other daughter didn't want to know anything. But she knew, because I remember being on the bed one day, and she was playing next to me. She had all of her dolls lined against the wall, and then she took one doll, and she threw it in the closet and she said, "We don't want to play with you. You have an ow-ey breast. We don't like ow-ey breasts." I couldn't hold her because I was in so much discomfort.

The overriding fear was that the damage to children would last forever. "There is a permanent scar on my kids," a survivor stated. "I had a doctor's appointment yesterday, and it was delayed. My daughter started to panic, so I made sure that I would stop the appointment and call and say, 'I'm late, and there is a long line at Kaiser and they're just inefficient.' She was thinking they must have found something bad." When a second woman finished treatment in 1993, her ten-year-old son "took the styrofoam head my wig sat on and put a firecracker on it and exploded it in the backyard": "I thought that was how he would be able to move on. But it didn't work out that way." Before graduating from high school eight years later, he went on a compulsory retreat. "A lot of the retreat was working on how he survived his mom being sick. I didn't realize he took it so hard until he came home, and he gave me his four-day journal." Jean Trawick was convinced her young son "got the brunt of it" when she underwent treatment. "He used to go with me to doctor appointments and destroy the waiting room; he was nine and ten at the time. He would throw all the furniture around and scream and throw tantrums, and I tried psychiatrists and psychologists with him, and they couldn't help." "Even now," Jean stressed, twenty years after her last chemotherapy infusion, he refused to discuss his experience.

"You're Fine. You're Cured"

Although the women reported greatly varying responses from the people in their social worlds during breast cancer treatment, a single theme dominated the discussion of the posttherapy period: whatever support previously had been available quickly evaporated. The friend who accompanied Pat Garland to chemotherapy withdrew as soon as it was over. So did the members of Rose Jensen's support network: "After my treatment a lot of people around me seemed to feel, 'You're fine. You're cured. You don't need anything. We don't want to hear about it anymore.' My kids didn't want to hear about it. My ex didn't want me going on about it." Leanne Thomas commented, "My sister was there, and she was supportive. She used to call me, and she doesn't call me anymore. I had a girlfriend that would call, and she doesn't call anymore. My father says, 'You're going to be OK. You are OK.' So I guess I'm supposed to be fine." Marge Barlow described her lover this way: "At first, she was very sympathetic, but then after treatment she wasn't. So it was like I'd say, 'I'm too tired to walk there,' and she'd say, 'Well you can't still be tired.'" Another woman told us, "My husband's attitude is, 'OK, you've had a mastectomy. You've had surgery. You've lived. Now what's your problem?'"

Even men who had undergone cancer expected the women to put their experiences behind them. "I want to tell you a story," one woman began. "A friend of mine, he had testicular cancer, and he's always asking how I am doing. I tell him that I am involved in my volunteer cancer things. He said, 'You know what, that's all you talk about. Can't you just let that go? I mean it's over and done with. Is that all you do?' He said, 'That's all you ever talk about. It's so depressing. Can't you just get out of it, just move on with your life, move on?'" A second woman spoke about her husband: "He had cancer when he was a boy and had part of his leg removed, and he thinks, 'Well I know, I had it too.'"

Women offered various explanations for the grudging support they received after treatment ended. The lack of a clear diagnosis may have convinced friends and family that the symptoms did not "really" exist. One woman believed that friends assumed their "job" was "to be a little bit in denial, to help you lift up." Marge Barlow pointed out that the symptoms served as a reminder to her social network as well as to herself that a life-threatening disease had struck and could return at any time: "People want me to say, 'Oh, yeah, I'm back and everything's fine.' It's less frightening for them. It's like when a couple that's your best friends break up. It shakes your relationship. That's kind of how I felt about having cancer in regard to everybody I know. It's very important for them that this is just over for me." Another survivor noted that her husband's life had narrowed along with hers. When fatigue prevented her from going out in the evening, he too stayed home. Others focused on the open-ended nature of the symptoms. Like the survivors, family and friends had counted the days until radiation and chemotherapy would stop. None had anticipated interminable side effects.

Perhaps another impediment to continued support was the survivors' ambivalence about requesting it. When we asked Rose Jensen how her symptoms had affected her relationship with her family and friends, she answered, "I try to not burden them with cancer talk. I filter." A second survivor took pains not to "make a big deal" about her fatigue: "My family, I don't really bug them about it." Similarly, Pat Garland was "very careful not to talk about anything on a continuous basis because that will run people away. I wait until it's really got me down before I mention it."

Women who disclosed ongoing problems tried to minimize them. When one woman confided her troubles to friends, they laughed because she "always" ended "the series of complaints with, 'But I'm not dead, so it's fine.'" Another woman used the negative example of a relative to explain her reluctance to reveal the full extent of her back pain:

> I talk about my back symptoms but I don't say, "Oh, I can't move. I can't do anything." I'm not like that in every conversation. They'll ask, "How's your back? Is it any better?" And I'll say, "Maybe just a little bit. But I'm going to try something better soon." I don't like to focus on that entirely because I know how that can be, because one of the people in my sphere, one of the cousins from back East who lives down in Florida, she's acquired this weird allergy stuff that she is allergic to everything. She almost looks like a bubble girl, where if you were wearing a certain kind of shampoo she couldn't stand it. It was awful. And she would talk about it constantly, and it got really annoying.

To some extent, of course, these women may have been responding to the cues they received from others. If friends laughed at the ritual closing statement, "I'm not dead," they also may have signaled their discomfort with an ongoing litany of complaints. One woman recalled that she "started to pick up vibes from the people [she] was depending on" that she was asking too much of them. But words like "burden" and "bug" and the anecdote about a "really annoying" cousin suggest that the survivors also were guided by their own notions of proper conduct. In a society that expects recovery from every illness to follow a linear pattern of progress, lingering health problems provoke guilt. Feeling unworthy of long-term support, the women censored themselves.

"To Feed off Their Strength"

Survivors were far more comfortable asking for help in support groups. Such groups have proliferated in Los Angeles, as in other parts of the country. The L.A. County Breast Health Research Guide lists twenty-five organizations providing support groups for breast cancer patients and survivors.[6] Because we recruited many members of our sample through those groups, it was unsurprising that a majority of the survivors we interviewed participated in them at least sporadically.

Leanne Thomas explained her decision to enroll this way:

> When I was diagnosed, after I had the lumpectomy, I was watching TV and I saw these black women, and they were all playing some type of ball together. They worked and all came together and practiced and did something. And they were supporting each other. I said, "Hmm, I need to do that." Prior to this I was a volunteer for the American Cancer Society, not knowing that this was going to happen to me. I would participate in their walks and all the events that they had. I had the number, and I said, "Let me call and say that I want to get a support group." They gave me one that was over my way. I wanted to get one that was more of my nationality so I could relate to them. So when they said, "Sisters," I said, "OK, that's it." They were older women, and they had been survivors for years, and they could tell me what to anticipate because I had never gone through this before, and I didn't know. . . . I wanted to talk to my mom, but she wasn't here. The next best thing that I could do was to get a support group.

Another woman joined a group "while going through the chemo to be with other people who had gone through the same thing [she] went through and to feed off their strength."

Breast cancer groups became even more critical after treatment, when other types of support receded. Pat Garland "looked to" her group "to replenish" her because she failed to "get replenished" in her "immediate environment." After telling us about the depression that assailed her two years after finishing treatment, a second woman exclaimed, "And thank God I had a place to kind of vent, a safe place where people would understand. Because your family and everybody else doesn't." A third survivor explained why she discussed her symptoms only with her support group: "Talking to other people was like talking to a wall."

Women who felt profoundly alone with their symptoms were relieved to discover they belonged to a community of sufferers. "As we talk about the struggles that we go through," one woman remarked, "we talk about the aches and the pains and the this and the that, and then we hear that other people are having those same struggles and aches and pains that you have. So we do that monthly, and it's a real source of strength." Another said, "A lot of times you get depressed, and you say, 'Why me?' And then you find out that there are quite a few other women that experienced the same thing, so I know I'm not alone." A third told us, "Every time I leave a meeting I gain something. I say, 'Oh, God, I'm one of those people. I've got the same symptoms.' You become a prisoner in your own body because you don't know somebody else has got it. But then you hear five or six of the people go, 'Girl, yeah.'"

A few groups provided instrumental as well as emotional support. "If I needed some finances or something," a survivor said, "I could always call G. [the support-group leader]. . . . If I was hungry or needed something, she'd get it for me." After a recurrence and a second round of chemotherapy left another woman too weak to do some of her housework, she realized she could rely on members of her group: "If I was to ask any one of them to help me clean my house, they would. . . . We all help each other."

But support groups were not for all. One woman was uncomfortable disclosing "personal feelings" to strangers: "I'm an only child, and I was raised to keep things to yourself." With two jobs and a small child at home, another woman could not afford to take the "long drive" from her home in Burbank to the Wellness Community in Santa Monica on a regular basis. Some survivors had attended just once or twice before quitting. One faulted the leaders: "I didn't find them to be particularly insightful, and one of them pushed me to talk about my incest, which I didn't appreciate." Another recoiled from the tensions that erupted. Others found the atmosphere too depressing. "There were all these really sick people," a woman commented, "and I just didn't want to be around people that were dying." And some survivors discovered that their differences from other members were too great to be overcome. An African American, for example, could not make common cause with the all-white group she encountered at the Wellness Community. The group visited by Rose Jensen consisted entirely of "older women who were concerned about the fact that they just bought an RV or they wanted to see their grandchildren graduate, when here I wanted to get my kids through elementary school."

Forming New Relationships

Nina Worth's dramatic story demonstrates that breast cancer occasionally can create opportunities for new intimate relationships. As mentioned earlier, after surviving Hodgkin's lymphoma in her twenties, Nina had assumed she would have to remain single. But while undergoing breast cancer treatment ten years later, she met her future husband. The wedding occurred a year after her therapy ended.

Far more commonly, however, breast cancer shattered hopes of finding new relationships. Sexual difficulties discouraged this single woman:

> I've realized the way I am with men now is quite different than the way I used to be. I mean I don't flirt the way I used to because I don't want it to go anywhere, because I'm afraid. It's really more fear of the physical discomfort than of an emotional connection, which is kind of sad now that I say it out loud. One of the sprinkler valves had a leak the other day, and a particular part was ripped broken, basically broken, and I just freaked out. . . . I just flipped out and

said, "That's it. I'm selling my house and I'm moving to an apartment. I can't deal with this. If I had a man around, then he could
fix it." And I called a gardening-helper guy who would sometimes
work for my sprinklers. I said, "I have an emergency. You have to
come over right now." And he came over and showed me what was
wrong, and I said that I was going to try to get a replacement before
the OSH store closes. That's Orchard Supply Hardware. So I roared
off and talked to the nice people there. They showed me what I
needed. This couple of screws, and I got them, and I fixed it, and I
was so proud of myself, and I said, "Calm down now, you don't have
to sell your house, because you fixed it." But what kept on coming
back was that if I had been living with somebody, I wouldn't have
freaked out like that, and I would've said, "Hey, you! Guy, fix this."

A recently separated woman said, "It would take a very understanding
spouse to deal with the issues that I have left over from the chemo and
with my memory and the cognitive stuff." As a result, she was "not even
looking." Although a teacher had tried to find a new relationship after
her first bout with breast cancer, she abandoned her search when the
disease returned:

> One of the things that was happening was I went to Parents without
> Partners, and I was dating guys who had kids who were in school.
> And I just thought I didn't want to get in a relationship with a child
> who had already lost a parent through divorce or widowhood or
> whatever and then get me in their life and then have something
> happen to me. It sounds really stupid, but I work with children, and
> I see how much children suffer from just the littlest things. And that
> was why when I got it the second time, I said, "I don't want to mess
> with those people with little kids," or medium kids, enough that
> they weren't out and independent like seniors in high school. I can't
> say I wrote that part of my life out as a conscious effort. It's hard to
> find places to go where you meet the right kind of guys at my age
> anyway, so a lot of it doesn't have to do with the cancer. But I would
> probably be more aggressive or assertive in trying to find people if
> I hadn't had that.

Above all, breast loss convinced women that dating no longer was an option. "It's like now," a divorced, forty-five-year-old woman told us, "I don't feel as beautiful. It's like I'm not as confident as I was before I had my breasts removed. I'm not as confident getting to know someone new in that way, not at all." When Pat Garland complained about the loneliness in her life, we asked if her mastectomy inhibited her from trying to find a mate. Her response: "Yes, oh yes! Oh most definitely! You don't walk into this thing, because the first thing you gotta do is tell them you're missing a breast. That's the first thing you've gotta get over and hope that they don't start running." Jean Trawick explained her reluctance to resume dating: "It's a real problem when I think about meeting a man and going, 'By the way, I don't have a breast.' It's kind of like, 'Goodness, I hope this doesn't progress to a romantic occurrence because I don't know what I'm going to do then.'" Annie Briggs refrained from looking for a partner because "everybody is not going to adjust to looking at your scar."

The Evaporation of Support

As our interviewees discovered, having an established group of social contacts does not automatically convert into social support. Some family members and friends withdrew as soon as the diagnoses became public. Many more dropped away when treatment side effects lasted for months and then years. We can explain these responses in various ways. Like the women themselves, close relatives were strongly influenced by the celebratory breast cancer culture, which seems to promise robust good health to all survivors. Some family members and friends thus may have doubted whether the women really were suffering as much as they claimed. Some also may have faulted the women for failing to recover from problems so many other survivors had surmounted. Moreover, it was one thing to provide help during the bounded treatment period; it would have been a very different matter to furnish sustained assistance indefinitely. As people increasingly confront chronic rather than acute illnesses, sickness has become a much lonelier experience.[7] It also is possible that the survivors inadvertently pushed people away. In the aftermath of trauma, it was all too easy to exaggerate slights. Feelings of shame about long-term symptoms probably discouraged many survivors from asking for the support they craved. Single women may have been too quick to stop dating.

The story was not uniformly grim. Receiving unanticipated forms of support, a few women gained a new understanding of the meaning of human connectedness. A male friend's care during treatment allowed Nina Worth to open herself to the possibility of a permanent attachment. And support groups partially compensated for the defaults of intimates. Nevertheless, a sense of loneliness and isolation pervaded the majority of interviews. When the women were most in need of affirmation, emotional sustenance, and practical assistance, little was forthcoming.

Studies of the patient perspective on illness note that experiences in one area commonly reinforce those in another.[8] The following chapter demonstrates that women whose symptoms led to an abandonment of jobs and leisure activities were especially likely to feel the absence of both affective and instrumental support. At the same time, withdrawal from work and social life compounded the feelings of marginalization many women had experienced since treatment began.

5

Narrowed Lives

ALTHOUGH ROSE JENSEN used to work as an engineer, she is now an office manager. Interviewed during two successive lunch hours, she began by explaining why she has a job far beneath her ambitions and qualifications:

> I went from someone who kept phenomenal amounts of very so-
> phisticated, concrete data in my head to someone who can't get out
> of the house in the morning without making a list. When I was di-
> agnosed I was the project manager for a twenty-four-million-dollar
> government project retrofitting military aircraft. I had thousands of
> engineering drawings and concepts in my head. I had names and
> phone numbers, figures—I had a mind like a steel trap. . . . I'm still
> probably more efficient than the average fool, but I know that I'm
> different, which is one of the reasons that I'm working here and not
> in a more responsible position. . . . This is a much less demanding
> job. I don't need to have the kind of technical expertise that I did in
> that position. I have the earning potential that's about twenty-five to
> thirty thousand dollars less. . . . And I have friends who have MBAs
> from UCLA like I do who say, "You could get a so much better job.
> You could do anything. You don't have to have a job at this salary.
> You're earning nothing." And I'm thinking, "You know what? I'm re-
> ally grateful to be earning anything at this point."

Given the type of work Rose did, the effects of "chemobrain" were especially devastating.

Her life started to unravel soon after her breast cancer diagnosis, when she quit her government job and claimed Social Security Disability Insurance. As a result, she noted, "our earning potential as a family went down so much we had to give up our home and move into a much more modest home. Not that we were in a mansion or anything. We started ratcheting down. And it was really hard on the girls. They were four and eight at the time." Medical bills compounded her financial difficulties. Although private insurance covered some of her treatment, her plan's high deductibles and copayments left her responsible for a significant share.

Her first foray back into the work world, in the midst of treatment, demonstrated how altered she was. Changes she could ignore at home became starkly apparent when she spent the day in an office:

> My neighbor, who is a consultant, used to ask me to help her, [and] because I wasn't working, she said, "Why don't you work in my office and, you know, see how you're doing?" And at the end of the day she'd say, "You know, Rose, you're not the person you used to be. If you don't write things down, you forget what I asked you to do, and you never used to do that." And, after weeks of forgetting things, she finally said, "You know I love you dearly, . . . but I can't ask you to do things that I used to be able to ask you and expect them to be done."

When chemotherapy ended and Rose was ready to work full-time, she found refuge in a job at an Internet company with relatively few intellectual demands and flexible hours:

> They would allow me to come and leave when I needed as long as I put in eight hours, because many of the people were telecommuting from their homes, which were all over. . . . And there was a couch there, and since I was the only one there, the attitude of one of the partners was, "If you need to lie down, fine. Just as long as you do the work, you do it well, and you're there for when we need you." And those were the parameters he set, and that's what I did.

But the business soon folded, and she was back on the job market. This time her priority was to find not only a position she could handle but also one with good health benefits: "When I was working at the Internet company, they were able to get me minimal insurance, but it wouldn't cover any kind of cancer treatments. And let's face it, I'm not really worried about getting the flu. And so insurance is what drove me. I looked only in government or university work, because [there would be] a big enough pool so that they couldn't discriminate on prior conditions." The job she found was at a cancer center connected to a large university.

A new blow fell a few years later, when her husband filed for divorce. She and the girls then moved into her mother's apartment, where Rose slept on the living-room couch. Although she welcomed her mother's child care, Rose lost her independence: "Someday I'd like my own room again because I'd like to put my things up. My tastes are unique enough that my mother doesn't like a lot of my things. I'm into folklore and masks and puppets, and she finds them frightening, some of my masks from Bali and some of the Mexican masks I've collected." Her life has shrunk in other ways as well. The cognitive impairments that stunted her career also restrict her social life: "I don't put myself in situations where I have to worry about my memory or ability. I don't think I'd go to a fancy party at the Music Center with my friend who is a composer even though she has invited me, because I don't think I'd be able to handle the conversation. I think I'm quieter than I used to be." And she reads much less than before: "I never really engaged in any kind of leisure activities, and I still don't, other than reading. . . . I can't read technical books anymore. I just don't understand them. I'll read the same page over and over and over again, and it just doesn't make sense. . . . I don't read philosophy books anymore. I don't read books about politics or historical analysis or critiques. My reading is a lot lighter."

Rose's trajectory has made a mockery of the celebratory breast cancer culture surrounding her. Asked to assess her life, she compared herself to the idealized image of the successful breast cancer survivor:

I'm not pursuing happiness. It's not like one of the beast cancer women who is climbing Annapurna and showing the world that I can do it. I feel kind of beaten down. I think I've gotten some pretty hard smacks. Part of it is the marriage, the home, the finances. So it's all those major life issues which for me were precipitated by the finding of the cancer. It's quite possible that the divorce and the moving out of the house would have happened eventually anyway, but I don't know that my financial situation would have been impacted if I had stayed in that career or been able to transfer to a comparable job. If so, I might have been able to have afforded a place of my own.

She concluded that cancer "was the card making the house of cards fall down."

Employment

The accidents of personal history partly explain why cancer wrought such havoc in Rose's life. Her marriage already was troubled when the disease struck. Although the union lasted another five years, her husband fled as soon as he was convinced she would survive. Forced to care for young children by herself, she decided her only option was to move in with her mother, thus sharply curtailing her independence. And yet, in its broad outline, Rose's story is by no means unique. Researchers find that, between one and five years after diagnosis, 20 percent of cancer survivors have physical limitations that restrict their employment opportunities; 9 percent cannot hold any type of job. Others reduce their hours or find less challenging jobs.[1]

Because we interviewed only women who self-identified as suffering from post-breast-cancer symptoms, it is unsurprising that a very high proportion had work-related problems: 12 percent considered themselves too disabled to hold any job; another 12 percent remained in the labor force but reported that their symptoms seriously affected their employment.

Like Rose, most women began by focusing on the months of chemotherapy, when they experienced pain, debility, nausea, and weakened immune systems. In one way Rose was extremely fortunate. When she had needed to quit work, she had been able to do so. Although her own income had plummeted, her husband's salary continued to sustain the household. Some women had no safety nets. Listening to other members of a focus group talk about relinquishing jobs while undergoing breast cancer therapy, Jean Trawick grew increasingly incensed. She finally interjected,

> I don't know about the rest of you—maybe you have a husband or somebody that is supporting you—but when I got cancer the first time, I was a single parent. I didn't have an option of not working. So I did all the radiation and all the cancer treatment while I was working and taking care of my kid. . . . My life just went on as if nothing happened. I went to radiation. I had a friend drop me off at the hospital. I continued working. I left on my lunch hour for radiation. And came back.

Perhaps because personal choice is so basic to autonomy, a quintessential American ideal, the other women tried to convince Jean her own decisions had been critical. One argued, "Well, you could have cried," to which Jean replied, "I did some of that, and that didn't make any difference. Nobody's going to pick up the pieces." When another woman said, "You could have fallen apart," Jean countered, "If I fell apart, I would have lost my son in court. I would have lost my job." Although two other participants insisted she had exercised choice by refusing to follow that route, she remained adamant: "No, it wasn't a choice. There was no choice. If you have options, you have choice."

But even women with real alternatives often stayed in the labor force. Jobs provided not only incomes but also stability, routine, a sense of self-worth, and personal fulfillment. A fund-raiser at a major cancer center, Nina Worth worked part-time to "maintain the semblance of a regular life in and around the times [she] was going for chemo." A nurse kept her job because she was "trying so desperately to have some normalcy" in her life. "It really helped." Although Marge Barlow was convinced she should have "dropped out of graduate school" as soon as she received her diagnosis, she explained, "I went ahead" partly because "my program gave me money to keep me afloat while I has sick" and partly because "it seemed important not to let cancer derail my plans." Tessa McKnight reported a similar mixture of motives:

> I own my own business, a flower shop, and it's a small business and it's something that I have to be there for, basically for it to run. I need to connect with my clients. So I did. I went to work. I worked pretty much though the whole thing, and I had weddings and stuff that were booked like way in advance before I knew that I was gonna have chemo or anything. So I had to do everything, which was good because I love my work, and it really kept me out of staying home and feeling sorry for myself. I had to get up and go to work. And I love flowers.

Two cultural ideals also helped to keep women at their jobs. One was the work ethic. An overriding fear of many women was that they would be regarded as malingerers, exploiting physical limitations to win exemption from work. The other was the Horatio Alger myth, which holds that success is available to anyone with enough willpower and pluck. Even missing a few days of work could make women consider themselves failures. An accountant recalled,

> I started chemotherapy in November, and the tax season starts in February. I asked Dr. S., "Would I be able to tell my office that I'll be back for tax season?" He said, "Oh, most likely, yes. We'll schedule you so that you can have chemotherapy on Friday, and you'll be back to work on Monday." I don't know what Monday it was because I was so violently ill. You know what that made me feel like? That there is something wrong with my will.

By the time of our interviews, several women had begun to reassess their determination to continue working throughout treatment. One, for example, said, "I didn't think I needed to have just stayed home all the way through the first year. That was my biggest mistake, because I should have." When asked what advice she had for women about to undergo breast cancer treatment, another survivor responded, "What I say to everybody that's going through it is, 'You'll never believe me, and you probably won't even do it, but if you can do one thing for yourself, just take a break.' Really, the natural thing is that you want to push yourself. They kind of make it like a heroic thing. People work, and if you don't happen to be one of those that can, then you say, 'What am I?' If you're not that hero, then what?"

The myth of the "strong black woman" was an additional burden on the African Americans in our study.[2] Pat Garland recalled,

> They gave me Adriamycin, but they said, "We'll only give you four treatments instead of the six." I thought, "Oh, no problem. I can work through this—no big deal." And I tried, and then after the second treatment my immune system literally crashed, and basically I had no immune system. So I had to go home and stay in bed for the next treatment. . . . When I went and did my chemotherapy, there was another black lady. She never stopped working. . . . That's what tripped me up because I kept saying, "Well, mine is small. My cancer's so small. I should be able to do this. People do this all the time."

Looking back over her experience, Pat urged other African Americans not to hold themselves to impossible standards:

> Those of us that were trying to teach African American women who thought that they were superwomen—you know, they could run home, and they could take care of the kids and do all these things— we were trying to teach them to take the cape off. And listen to their bodies. That was more important than being superwoman. . . . It's OK to complain. It is OK to feel bad. It's OK to acknowledge that you are so doggone tired that you can't go to work. That does not make you a failure.

Pat also tried to spread her message to the medical community:

> I went to so many seminars, and the response to chemotherapy was, "Make them get out of bed." I stood up. I said, "You know, I'm not

educated. I don't have a degree in anything. But I do have the experience of chemotherapy, and I would want to shoot somebody if I
was laying in bed with chemotherapy and they told me I better get
up because I'm depressed. I'd be ready to shoot 'em because no matter how much I wanted to, my body couldn't do it."

It was far easier for women to release themselves retrospectively
from work obligations during treatment than to accept that the lingering effects of that treatment would affect their employment situations
for years, possibly forever. Even those who cut back their hours or quit
their jobs entirely had assumed their careers would be back on track
once chemotherapy and radiation ended. Rose Jensen was not alone in
her disappointment. Altered appearance dimmed a teacher's hopes of
advancement: "I have not been able to wear a prosthesis without my
arm at least feeling like it is swelling up and hurting. And I am afraid to
push it too far. So I can only wear loose clothes. So far I haven't been
brave enough to do reconstruction because I have been hearing a lot of
negative things about it, and I am kind of afraid to mess up what's going
well. And of course, that is affecting my career too, because I want to
move into administration and I can't do that." When asked if her attire
was really what held her back, she responded, "Yes, the way I dress. You
would have to dress more professionally. Sounds like a little thing—but
this is one thing that weighs big on me."

An inability to handle pressure was a far more common problem. A
woman in a managerial position recalled,

> I had kind of made myself promise, because of the stress of the job,
> that I was going to cut down. And the first six months back I really
> did, and I didn't let it get to me. Then pretty soon you start look-
> ing better and people just expect you to do more, and being a first-
> born, I never knew how to say no. And I think what was happening
> was that the promise I made to myself to take care of myself and to
> nurture me wasn't happening. So I started getting more stressed at
> work. And finally, August the twenty-third, we just got through an
> audit. And I said to myself, "I have to make it through the audit." I
> pleaded with the Lord and everybody else, "Give me strength to get

through the audit so that we know everything is fine." And when I went to work on that Friday, I just sat there and I started crying, and that's not me. I have a very good primary-care doctor, and I called her. And I think she just heard from my voice or whatever—she said, "Get in here." So I went right away, and she said, "I am putting you on leave right now." So I did it for like three weeks, and I was kind of better.

Although stress often is viewed as the province of workers in high-status jobs, it may be especially intense at the bottom of the occupational hierarchy.[3] A clerical worker said, "Anytime I'm timed and rushed, that's fatiguing for me. 'Hurry up and do this. Hurry and do that.' I come home after work, and I really feel drained." Studies reporting that stress can harm the immune system suggest that the women's jobs may have imperiled their health, even as the symptoms undermined their employment.[4]

The effect of other symptoms varied by type of employment. Fatigue and pain were especially serious problems for women in positions demanding physical labor. "One thing is real important for people to understand," a survivor commented. "I identified myself as a registered nurse. I am a labor and delivery nurse." No longer "strong enough" to work twelve-hour days, however, she decided to "throw in the towel." Two other survivors who quit physically taxing jobs focused on the economic repercussions. A divorced woman responsible for two nieces saw her income drop "way down, almost 80 percent." A massage therapist left her practice first to undergo radiation and then to nurse her terminally ill husband. "For most of my life I have been extremely strong," she remarked. "You can see my muscle structure is good." When her husband died a year after her own treatment ended, she anticipated no problems resuming work and making the money she and her nine-year-old son desperately needed:

> I thought, "Well, OK, I can start work again. I can do massage therapy, which I love and which I've done for twenty-five years." All of a sudden I would get so weak I could hardly finish an appointment. I'd try to do my clients, who, you know, are friends as well as clients, and I just felt more and more frustrated. I was afraid of scheduling

appointments because I was afraid to either not do a good job or not be able to finish, or I was afraid of the pain that I had the day after I'd do the massages.

Hoping that the California sun would help, she had traveled from her home in Oregon to Los Angeles for a vacation. But her pain became worse instead of better, and when we interviewed her, she had earned no income for several months.

A professor also testified to the impact of pain on her work life. She spent her one-hour commute with an ice pack wrapped around her back "just to make it numb" so she could "bear it": "By the time I get there I can barely get out of my car and straighten out." Coping with pain also made her job "more difficult" during the long day ahead: "Sometimes I have to lie down on the floor in my office. If I'm in a meeting, I'm always moving and having a hard time with it. It affects my enjoyment with my job. I like what I do, but if I'm in pain a lot of the time, I just can't wait to get home."

Above all, cognitive dysfunction impeded professional, managerial, and clerical employment. "I could talk [about] chemobrain," a legal secretary said:

> I was sort of given a job mercifully by a former employer, who set me up with a nice job in the mayor's office in city hall in Los Angeles, and I was in charge of some of the blue-ribbon committees. I was supposed to be facilitating the moving and getting all these important people together in one room at the same time, helping with whatever project they were working on, making sure they had the paperwork that they needed and everything was running smoothly—basically a lot of logistic stuff. And I had to use—I had to learn to use Word, and I had to use an Apple computer that I have never used before. I had the hardest time, and I can remember just sitting there and thinking, "My brain is just absolutely dead. I don't think I'll ever be able to think again," and finding it very frightening.

After a year she returned to the law firm where she had worked prior to her diagnosis: "I wanted to do something familiar I knew I could do. Especially after having that year when I was doing things that I really wasn't sure what I was doing. So I thought, 'I'll just go back and do something that I'm familiar with in case my chemobrain doesn't go away.'" Because a clerk-typist had changed jobs "several times" since completing treatment seventeen years earlier, she repeatedly had confronted her limitations:

> When you're used to doing a job on a daily basis you have it down pat. This job I've been doing for about three years. I'm still learning the ends and odds about it, but I feel that I should have been here long enough at this job title to know exactly what I'm doing. Sometimes I have to call downtown [to headquarters] to make sure that I'm doing the right thing so that I won't make an error. Sometimes I go and do things and then I say, "Oh, I made a mistake." Then I have to call downtown, and they have to get me out of it.

Others had new problems with concentration. When a teacher returned to the classroom, she was dismayed to find herself distracted whenever someone walked down the hall. A psychologist complained, "I don't have the same powers of concentration. I tend to work on something, and my mind just wanders. It's since I've come back to work." A woman responsible for typing doctors' notes at a hospital stated, "Being a transcriptionist, I better know what these people are saying. I try to concentrate as much as I can. I have to because my job is too important." Paying attention to the words on the dictaphone, however, had become much harder than before.

In chapter 3 we noted the various ways women tried to hide cognitive difficulties at work. But concealment was not always possible. When a legal secretary called "downtown" for help correcting a "mistake," she exposed her problems to her supervisors. After Greta Shaw finally changed jobs, she realized that her new colleagues regarded her as "kind of dumb." Even worse, her position required constant interaction with customers:

> Oh, it just can be really embarrassing. I mean I can almost be helping someone, and then I just walk away and I'll start doing

something else and I'll forget that they're even there. I'm like, "Oh my God! I can't believe I forgot." And I do it a lot. That's just bizarre. I mean that's like, whoa! I am really a customer-service oriented type of person, and I really care what people think. For me it's like horrible. It's like, "I am not that kind of a person! I am not a flake! Trust me!"

A court clerk's deficits also frequently were on display: "I'm at the counter and I'm working on doing filing, then all of a sudden I draw a blank, like, 'What do I do next? Am I supposed to stamp this document or not?' And I go to my notes to check it out, instead of going bam, bam, bam." An accountant found it impossible to "get away" with her "problem recalling the right words": "If someone comes in and you're going over their taxes, you can't just say, 'Well, let's do code number XYZ and blah, blah, blah.' They say, 'Wait a minute, I'm going to find somebody else who will speak English to me.'" As a fund-raiser, Nina Worth "had always been really good at remembering people's names." But now, she said, "When I would see board members or donors, I would recognize their faces, but I couldn't for the life of me get their name back out. I had to figure out ways to work around that, given that you don't always have name tags on at events."

Public performances were fraught with new difficulties. As related earlier, Marge Barlow had practiced law for several years before returning to school to get a doctorate in history. Now she was looking for an academic job:

> It's extremely stressful to go to interviews knowing that I have these memory issues. I'm just not as sharp as I was. I used to be a litigator, and I used to be able to think on my feet really well. People always say things like, "When you're on trial, do you take breaks to go to the bathroom?" And I'm like "NO! You just sit there. You don't even think about going to the bathroom. You're just focused." But that's gone, that edge is just totally gone now.

A woman who still worked as an attorney said, "At times I'm not as quick in court, and I think, 'Why didn't I think about doing blah, blah,

blah?' That scares me. And I know it's because the mental capability isn't how it used to be." Another lawyer suddenly had to write "everything down" before making "significant speeches and presentations." Otherwise she "would be up there talking and it's flowing, and all of a sudden it's blank."

Like Rose Jensen, some women with cognitive limitations lowered their aspirations, refusing to apply for more challenging jobs. Several others retired early. An oncology nurse "used to thrive under stress": as the coordinator "of a thirty-six-unit ward, I was used to having to channel twenty or more things, and that was a piece of cake. I loved it because it was kind of a thrill and was exciting for me." But that "thrill" and excitement turned to anxiety and anguish after cancer. Now she "had to do things linearly. I have to take things slowly, and I have to do things one thing at a time." Although she twice returned to work, "something happened that made me aware that I was a danger to my patients. There was a patient who died who wouldn't have died. And I knew that it would not have happened with my old self, and I thought to myself, 'I knew my memory was not good enough.' There is a million things that you have to remember. I couldn't be running around with all these hundred of pieces of paper."

Ida Jaffe explained her decision:

> I had a really good job. I loved my job; I worked with good people. I wasn't even looking forward to retirement. Before cancer I would have probably worked until I was about sixty or sixty-five, and I enjoyed it. I went into retirement because of the cancer, simply because I could not maintain the level of work that I was used to, because I was responsible for a lot at work. I was not the office manager, but I was held like the office manager. They came to me for everything. I had a big responsibility, and I enjoyed it. It was a high-powered job, and therefore, after the cancer and going back to work, I couldn't sustain that. Every two hours I was going somewhere to sit down and relax and could not think well. I couldn't coordinate everything that was going on. I was basically the coordinator, and I knew where everything was, and I kept everything flowing. I couldn't do it anymore. With this memory thing I was very frustrated at work, and

so I thought that I can't go on like this. It was a chore now going to work rather than a joy. I just assessed the situation and said that it's not worth it.

Asked how she felt about her departure from the labor force, she said, "The realization that I couldn't go back to work was devastating. I was in my early forties, so it was like something was taken away from me, not so much the breast, but my life was taken away from me."

Accommodations

The 1990 passage of the Americans with Disabilities Act (ADA) required employers to make "reasonable accommodations" for disabled people who are "otherwise qualified" for their jobs. In our study, that law was notable primarily by its absence. One reason may be that the women we interviewed typically shied away from viewing themselves as disabled. Still struggling to restore their precancer selves, they held themselves apart from the millions of other people experiencing physical or mental impairments. Another reason may be that the law has had little impact. Survivors who knew about the ADA would have learned that the courts have interpreted it extremely narrowly and that it therefore serves very few people. The greatest problem claimants face has been an inability to convince the court that a mental or physical condition represents a disability, a particularly serious obstacle for the many survivors with poorly understood symptoms.[5]

Of course, legal pressure is not always necessary to convince employers to do the right thing. "I'm very blessed to have a job that's very understanding," commented an employee-transportation coordinator. "My boss's wife went through breast cancer a year before me. When I do my Revlon Walk, they are very supportive. 'You're doing a good thing.' This is something that they can give back to something they believe in. They're very supportive of me. I try not to abuse the situation and everything. I'm just so blessed that people look at me as a miracle." Despite serious, persistent fatigue, a second woman was able to keep her job by rearranging her work schedule:

I have a wonderful manager at work. It's not in the schedule, but I work a split shift. I'll go in from six to maybe until ten or eleven. I'll go home and then take a shower, lay down, and then I usually go back when everyone else is getting off. I'm single, my daughter is away in college, so I tell them I don't have a husband to get home to and cook for. When I wash, I wash. So I could go in and work from six to ten and then back at four, and I could work to six, seven at night or whatever time that will work for me. And my manager, as long as the work gets out, then that's fine.

Most bosses, however, refused to make special allowances. Far from smoothing a teacher's reentry to the classroom after the end of treatment, the principal demanded that she make up for lost time: "He saved all the extra chores that teachers do for me for when I came back rather than give them to the sub, and so I had to do ten months of extra chores on top of teaching." She was at a different school when she had a recurrence:

It was probably eight weeks into the year when I went out again, and [the principal] was not a real happy camper with me. Everything was fine until it was time to come back the next fall. And she had three openings: one was in the fourth grade, one was in fifth grade, and one was a fourth- and fifth-grade combination class, which is always way harder to teach. And she wouldn't give me the fourth grade. She would not give me the fifth grade. She said, "If you are good enough to come back, you are good enough to come back to the fourth and fifth; otherwise wait." And I could have gone to the district and the local union and gotten the position I wanted, but I thought, "I don't want to work for somebody that doesn't want me," and I hadn't been there long enough for her to really know what I could do. And so they transferred me to a second grade at another school.

Other women suffered more serious sanctions. Two, for example, saw themselves passed over for the promotions they believed would easily have been theirs had they not experienced posttreatment symptoms.

Even women who received special consideration realized it was strictly limited. Although grateful for the boss who facilitated her labor-force participation, the transportation coordinator took care "not to abuse" her "situation." After noting that she worked for "a pretty great group of women," who were "somewhat understanding" of her memory loss, Greta Shaw added, "but, you know, it's a business." The primary responsibility for accommodating her limitations, she believed, thus fell to her alone.

Insurance Concerns

Health insurance was another major issue for the women in this study. Rose was one of many who suddenly realized that most private coverage no longer provides adequate protection against large health care expenses. Because plans increasingly shift costs onto patients through high deductibles and copayments, hefty medical bills accumulate.[6]

Insurance also caused enormous difficulties for women who tried to change jobs after cancer diagnoses. It is easy to understand why Rose stated that health insurance "drove" her job search. In the United States, most people receive private health insurance either through their own employment or a family member's. A small proportion obtain coverage through individual plans; because employers make no contribution, however, those plans tend to be very expensive, and most exclude people with preexisting conditions, including breast cancer. Rose was well aware that small employers view cancer survivors as economic risks; should the disease return, the costs of care easily could overwhelm the group medical plan or lead to an increase in premiums. Rose thus had applied only to universities and government agencies, both of which had large risk pools. Moreover, she now needed "good" insurance rather than the "minimal" plan the Internet company offered; as she stressed, "the flu" was hardly her primary worry. Recent studies substantiate her concern; cancer survivors without adequate coverage are less likely than others to receive timely care and thus are more likely to have poor outcomes.[7]

Greta Shaw described health coverage as a "huge, tremendous weight on my shoulders." In her case, insurance constrained exit from the workforce rather than entry into it. Because her employment provided coverage for the entire family, she had taken a temporary leave rather than quit to undergo cancer treatment. When the leave had expired in the middle of radiation, she had returned to work before she felt ready. Now memory loss made the job even more difficult and less pleasurable, but she still could not contemplate retirement: "Our insurance is crucial, and for me especially. I have to have insurance, and I have to have good insurance. And that's where the insurance is from, so I've gotta work."

Access to life insurance also locked survivors into positions they yearned to escape. The group policy one woman obtained through her employment seemed especially vital for "the first few years after surgery, when I didn't know whether I was going to live or die. I felt that I had to cover my family so I can relax and stop worrying about it." But she was also "tired" of her job at Wells Fargo Bank:

> I wanted to quit so badly because I wanted a career again. I thought I was still young enough to qualify for a career. Because, see, I'm rethinking my thoughts, rethinking. I need a career. This is a stupid job I got here. . . . So I look around, calling insurance companies to see if they would qualify me for insurance. Couldn't find any. Finally got somebody to come out and give me a quote for the insurance policy, and my oncologist sabotaged me. He said that "some guy called and wanted to talk about your health." I said, "Fine, tell him the truth [about the cancer diagnosis]." So he tells the truth, and I didn't get the insurance.

As a result, she remained at her job.

Housework

Although the women in our study were far more likely to stress the effect of symptoms on paid employment than on domestic chores, a few noted that housework suffered. "Before, I would wash my own walls and go outside and wash the windows," Ida Jaffe told us. Now she either relied on her husband or left those tasks undone. Marsha Dixler noted, "I can't clean the bathtub and the shower because of me having the bilateral [mastectomy]." Fatigue had slowed her down: "It takes me much longer to do day-to-day housework. I have to do so much and, again, sit down. A lot of times when I sit down, it's hard to get back up and start again. I used to go nonstop and get the house cleaned." Women who had taken pride in the meticulous cleanliness of their homes felt the change especially keenly. "I'm not as energetic as I used to be about caring for the house," one said. "I was just a clean fanatic. I can't do that anymore, and I don't try it. It does upset me that I don't do it the way I used to." Another remarked, "I looked at my floor, and I said, 'Oh, my God.' I could eat off of my floor at one time." If house cleaning was a burden, it was also a source of self-esteem, and both women mourned its loss.

Leisure

As Rose discovered, postcancer symptoms disrupt leisure as well as work. Unable to concentrate as well as she could before, she abandoned the technical reading that previously had filled many evenings. Lymphedema, pain, and fatigue prevented other survivors from engaging in a host of physical activities, including jogging, racquetball, tennis, skiing, bicycle riding, bowling, golf, and dancing. The impact on one woman's family life was especially profound:

> I have two nine-year-old boys, so I'd like to do more. I will not go skiing with them. I would like to go skiing, but I'm petrified to go skiing. And when I go out and play ball with them I think, "Should I do this or should I not?" I think that I can throw my back out if I throw my football. So that's bothersome to me. I do take them to the beach. I don't jump in the water as much because I'm afraid if a wave hits me. So I'm much more tentative, and for a tomboy-type person who was always very athletic, it really pisses me off.
>
> My husband has a sailboat. I don't ever go on it because I'm afraid. It is a frustration because I don't like to be stopped from

doing anything. Just the thought that I have to think about, Should
I do this or not? Should I go on a motorboat? No, I shouldn't because if you slap down on a wave, you can really hurt your back,
and it would torture me. . . . And my husband will say, "Let's do
so and so." and I'll just look at him, "Honey, how can I do that?"
"Let's go play tennis." "I can't do that."

Two women curtailed their travels. One decided to avoid the "hot,
dry climates," which might cause her lymphedema to "blow up." When
the other remained severely fatigued several years after chemotherapy,
she realized, "There are things that I used to do and liked to do that I
probably won't do anymore. Like this weekend, my nephew got married in Cabo, and I had plans to go, and then I canceled my plans to go
because I felt it would be too much for me. Normally I would go and I
wouldn't care, but I felt like I couldn't do it—you know, getting ready,
preparation, getting to the airport. So I do cut a little. I have, and I have
to."

When full-time jobs depleted limited energy reserves, women withdrew from more routine social activities. "Even just going and meeting friends" was impossible for an administrator: "I have to commute
to work, attend to a very stressful job, commute home. All I can do is
climb the stairs and go to bed. By the time everyone gets together, I'm
ready to take a nap or go to bed. That's not a full life to me." Another
administrator remarked, "If I work all day, towards the end of the week,
as Wednesday and Thursday and Friday come along, I run out of steam.
I can't go out to dinner after work. I work long hours, and I get off at
six or six thirty, so to go out and socialize after that, I don't have the
energy."

Memory loss compounded difficulties. We saw that Rose rejected
an invitation to the Music Center party because she doubted her ability to engage even in casual conversation. A nurse's social life also had
dwindled after breast cancer. Friends who could not understand her
ongoing complaints about lingering symptoms gradually dropped away.
Others had been work colleagues and lost touch when she was forced
to take early retirement. Now she devoted her days to art, but that was
"a solitary thing," and she was a "social" person. As a result, she enrolled

in an art class: "The class was sixteen weeks long, and I hear a person's name, and every week I come back I have to ask them again. I'll write it down, and I'll try to remember to go check the name before I go to the class so I'll remember it. Or I'll take the slip and put it in the car, so I have it with me, so before I walk in I have the name and I can walk in and know the person's name. It's a lot of work." When a misunderstanding initially threatened the one relationship with a classmate that seemed likely to blossom into a friendship, she realized she also had to devote "a lot of work" to both the timing and manner of disclosure:

> She had me over for dinner, and I was supposed to cook something, and I came the day after instead of the night of. I walk in and say, "Hi, everybody." And because it was an early thing in the relationship she had thought that I was standing her up and that I wasn't really interested. The problem is, you don't want to meet somebody and have to tell them your whole life story so that they'll be able to figure you out. But there are kind of critical things that if you want to have a friendship, you have to let people know. I'm still learning to find a way to do that with a sense of humor and lightness.

This woman performed a delicate balance. Had she revealed her mental problems too early, she might have frightened away a potential friend. But withholding that information also involved risk. And should she ever disclose her difficulties, she would have to "find a way" to do so with "humor and lightness," softening the impact on others and thus perhaps depriving herself of the sympathy and support she craved. Such delicate mastery of social cues represents yet another burden she had not shouldered before.

Contracting Horizons

Although many breast cancer patients relinquish workplace obligations during treatment, most expect to be well enough to fulfill their responsibilities after it ends. A substantial proportion, however, remain too disabled to do so. Those who either retire early, accept positions beneath their educational qualifications, or forfeit promotions experience serious economic repercussions. Although we could not quantify the extent of the financial loss, our interviews suggest it is substantial. Rose Jensen's salary declined nearly thirty thousand dollars annually. A divorced woman with two young nieces to support saw her income drop 80 percent. But the costs of disrupted work lives could not be measured in dollars alone. One nurse lost a central component of her self-definition when she realized that she was no longer able to do her job. Another told us that her social world contracted when she severed contact with former colleagues. Ida Jaffe felt as if her entire life had been "taken away."

Women who spoke about their lives as narrowing typically meant much more than that work had suffered. Although the dominant image of the breast cancer survivor today is a woman striding along in the Avon Corporation's three-day fund-raising walk or running ahead of the pack in the Susan G. Komen Race for the Cure®, many women in our study had to surrender all physically strenuous activities. Others sacrificed vacations and evenings with friends. And many discovered that withdrawal from both work and social activities magnified the deep sense of isolation they had experienced since diagnosis. Two problems this chapter recounts, the continuing burden of medical bills and difficulties obtaining health and life insurance, affect survivors regardless of the extent to which they experience posttreatment symptoms. Lingering complaints, however, may amplify the impact of both. Survivors like Rose, who no longer can command high salaries, find medical bills far more onerous than anticipated. The "job lock" created by insurance constraints represents an especially serious hurdle for those who no longer can perform their previous jobs. Although memory problems undermined Greta Shaw's work performance, she could not contemplate retirement as long as her family continued to rely on the insurance her employment provided.

And yet, as the next chapter shows, the breast cancer experience is not uniformly bleak—even when persistent symptoms prevent triumphal narratives. Although many of our interviewees initially protested the widespread insistence that they use illness as an occasion for inner growth, several gradually discovered the possibility of personal transformation through an acceptance of the inevitability of vulnerability.

6

"Turning a Bad Experience into Something Good"

BECAUSE MARGE BARLOW was writing a Ph.D. dissertation while undergoing breast cancer therapy, her memory loss was especially troubling. But during our long conversation in her tiny Craftsman-style house, we realized that she is more likely to be derailed by an expanded sense of self than by a diminished one. Following many other women, she emphasized the impact of a breast cancer diagnosis. In her case, it had not been all bad. "Let me backtrack," she began:

> The six months preceding my diagnosis were the worst period of my life emotionally. I had the dissertation I was working on, I had had a terrible breakup, Los Angeles was not working for me, and I was really fragmenting mentally. I was getting antidepressants from a psychiatrist, and I could tell that she didn't know what else to do for me. And I got the diagnosis, and literally the next day, I was totally together again. The depression was gone, the fragmentation was gone, I was totally on the spot. I organized my life. I called my mother, with whom I am estranged. She came. I said, "I might have to have a mastectomy next Friday. I need to prepare for the worst." I made a new will. I went to the bank. I put my mother on my accounts—all these very practical things. I bought a little portable CD player and books on tape so that I could lie in bed . . .
>
> And then the following week when we went to the doctor, the prognosis was less dire. I was very nervous because I had to rely on my mother. I had very few friends in Los Angeles. I had no money.

But I just stepped right up to the plate, and in many ways it was the best time in my life. I mean, I was not depressed the whole time. I was very confident. I'm not a spiritual person, but I just felt everything was going to be all right. The morning of my surgery, I just took a cab to the hospital. It was just like, "OK, this day is here, and now I'll know."

Treatment, too, had positive features:

It was interesting to not be working, to have no obligations, to be able to sit all day and do nothing. My relationship with time changed so dramatically, and an hour became so interesting, whereas before time either flew or there wasn't enough time in the day. And people would come over to bring me food so I would eat. I ate very little, but it was just such a pleasure, these little minutes. It was really such a change, and I just loved it. . . . It was also interesting to see the world of the sick. I had had a lot of friends who had been sick and died, but I hadn't spent great periods of time in a hospital, or outside a single patient's room. So it was very unusual for me to be in the big chemo room, where there's all these people getting chemo at one time. . . . It was a really interesting glimpse of the other world, of the sick.

When treatment ended,

I didn't really know if I wanted to be back in the world of the well. I didn't want to be back in my old life, up at five, working until eleven. Everybody's telling me these things about how stress contributes to cancer. I'm thinking, "I'm not going to blame myself for my cancer, but how do I become not stressed?" And people are saying all these things about how this is a wake-up call, and now you should change your life. And I resented that, and it made me angry because I had just changed my life. I quit fifteen years as a lawyer, went to graduate school, moved to this goddamned L.A., and now they're saying this is a blessing. I thought, "This is ridiculous." That's one reason I stopped going to the support group, because all these people are saying, "It's the luckiest thing. Now I have an opportunity to think about my life." And I think you should think about your life anyway. I didn't understand what I was supposed to do with this "experience," and what does this mean for me? Finally I just got to a place where I just thought, "Well, I'm not going to wake up with some enlightened idea, but I'm going to see how my life unfolds in a different way now." And that just requires a sort of different kind of self-consciousness and patience.

Although a dominant response to breast cancer is to try to reassert predictability and control, in Marge's case, illness produced the opposite—an awareness of the need to accept contingency and change.

Even while waiting to see what life would bring, however, Marge had to make a major career decision. Before she entered graduate school, her "backup plan" was public school teaching. Although she finally finished her dissertation the year after treatment and began writing the book she would need for a tenure-track job, she also obtained a teaching credential. By the time we interviewed her, Marge had been teaching high school history for three years while applying for assistant professor positions. She realized the choice might not be hers to make. Academic jobs are notoriously hard to find, and, although she had been selected as a finalist for several, she had yet to receive an offer. Nevertheless, she wanted to determine her own direction.

Ongoing mental and physical problems increased the attractiveness of high school teaching. Academia, she pointed out, is "a very competitive field, in which you must rely on your mental agility." Although she continually "pushes" herself, "trying to read and focus," she described herself as "very insecure when talking to people professionally because I'm worried I'm just going to draw a blank." Moreover, at forty-nine, she wondered if her energy level (also reduced from chemotherapy and radiation) could improve significantly. Her basic dilemma, however, was deciding whether she wanted to work as an academic, not whether she could. "How do I get time for those things that I miss now about being in the world of the sick?" she asked.

I've realized how badly I felt about all the things I'd given up while I was getting my Ph.D. Before I moved here I had four gardens, and I gardened at least one full day every weekend, if not both days. I had a vast social life. I was involved in a lot of things. And graduate school was so restricting, and my life became so narrow. When I got sick, I thought, "My God, I've spent four years doing one thing at the expense of everything else that's been so important to me." I wasn't sure that if I pursued an academic life that I would be able to still go back to those things that had been important, that I had just put aside, thinking it was temporary. It dawned on me it might not be temporary. For some people, the thought of walking away from a Ph.D. is unthinkable. But it's not to me. I don't think I would ever have thought this if I had not gotten sick. I never would have. I was just marching on one path as fast as I could.

The Quest for Meaning

Women repeatedly told us that they both resented the pressure to use illness as an occasion for inner transformation and welcomed the opportunity to reassess their lives. The pressure came from various sources. The underlying premise of the iconic Christian story is that good can emerge from personal defeat, suffering, and physical pain. Friends, relatives, and occasionally even acquaintances reassured newly diagnosed patients that they ultimately would find illness a blessing in disguise. Those who turned to the rapidly expanding genre of illness narratives undoubtedly received the same message. According to Arthur W. Frank, many of these narratives are "quest stories"; the "quest is defined by the ill person's belief that something is to be gained through the experience."[1] Anne Hunsaker Hawkins observes that the "pathographies" of people who have experienced heart attacks closely resemble seventeenth-century autobiographies of religious conversion. Both describe a "dramatic event that precipitates a profound change from one set of values to another and a concomitant transformation in life-style."[2] Similarly, Daniel Wilson concludes that the memoirs of mid-twentieth-century polio patients typically conform to the model of triumph narratives. Despite the rigid therapeutic regime to which they were subjected, most patients eventually were forced to acknowledge that they would have to live with some degree of impairment. Nevertheless, the authors were able to find meaning in their experiences and thus ultimately transcend them.[3] Diane Price Herndl notes that the authors of contemporary breast cancer narratives typically display a "deep need to make some sort of meaning out of experience."[4]

When a belief in the possibility of redemption through illness becomes a moral imperative, however, it infuriates rather than inspires. Two recently published breast cancer memoirs rail against the relentlessly upbeat cancer culture survivors encounter. One is Barbara Ehrenreich's article, discussed in the introduction. Chief among her targets are the following testimonials in a recent volume about the year after breast cancer: "'I can honestly say I am happier now than I have ever been in my life—even before the breast cancer.' 'For me, breast cancer has provided a good kick in the rear to get me started rethinking my life.' 'I have come out stronger, with a new sense of priorities.'"[5] Kathlyn Conway opens her unflinching account with a warning to the reader not to expect a reassuring story of hope and renewal: "I have maintained that the experience of cancer is without redeeming value; that I have not been transformed by the experience; that it is, beyond all else, a misery to be endured."[6]

Several women in our study spoke in a similar vein. Having recently moved across the country to embark on a new career, Marge "resented" the chorus demanding that she view her illness as a "wake-up call." A teacher pointed out that disease can debase as well as ennoble: "I get so mad when people say, 'I'm so glad I had breast cancer. It was such a great experience, and it's changed my life.' And I thought, 'Not mine!' I would be just as happy without it. I would probably be a better person without it. I think it made me a worse person." A secretary recalled the hollow ring of the words of consolation her doctor offered in their initial meeting:

> He said, "You can't understand this now. But all of my patients have said afterwards that having breast cancer was the most important, most significant event in their lives, and their lives are better afterwards," something like that. I just looked at him like he was nuts.

This little cocky man with a very expensive suit, and I thought, "You are just full of it. Who do you think you are to tell me that breast cancer is the best thing that ever happened to me?"

One survivor confronted a particularly persistent acquaintance:

A woman who I used to socialize with, whenever I used to see her, she'd tell me how blessed I was. I was in a rage. I was in a fucking rage. God gave me this disease, and now it should bring me closer to God and something wonderful would happen. I've told her a couple of times, "This really hurts my feelings. Please don't do this. It's difficult for me to see you socially," everything I could logically think of. But every time I'd see her, she lays this on me, but more strongly. So then I said, "You know, this really makes me feel sad because I don't think God would do that. God gives cancers to little babies, and I don't think God is that kind of person that would have you suffer so horribly to do something good. I just don't think God works that way." "Well, God's a mystery," was her answer. So then, finally, I said to her, "You know, I have you on my prayer list. I pray you get cancer so you can see the wonderful happiness and goodness that comes out of this." She still does it though.

Nevertheless, many women who most vehemently opposed the belief that breast cancer could engender inner growth gradually embraced that notion. Eighteen months after her diagnosis, the secretary told her "cocky" physician he had been "so right." Another woman said,

I have this one friend who went to the Wellness Community [a local support group], and it was the first time and everyone's going around and these women are saying, "Oh, breast cancer is the best thing that ever happened to me." And she was just so mad, she couldn't keep from screaming at them. And a few years later she said, "You know breast cancer really was the best thing," and I said, "You are not going to go there." But I learned there are valuable things.

One of those "valuable things" was the discovery of inner resources she never realized she possessed. The cancer ordeal "made me understand my own strengths by dealing with it the way I did." When we commented, "It's certainly a challenge," she responded, "Yeah, a big challenge, and I did it and I did it well."

Women also had a new appreciation for the external sources of support that had helped sustain them. Thus, survivors who had drawn on religion or spirituality during treatment often redoubled their faith commitments afterward. One noted that her religious practice had grown "stronger, very much stronger": "I remember I had a lot of fears, and I just handed them over to God, not knowing what would happen. I was really alone. God works through people. . . . So I've become very close. It's a good feeling. It actually feels like you're in this world, but you're in a peaceful part of this world." Religion helped Tessa McKnight deal with the profound questions illness provoked. When we asked if she changed her spiritual practices in response to cancer, she answered, "I'd already been really involved, and I was just glad that I already had what I had. I kind of felt like I had a deeper understanding about what life was about and even what death was about, because at some point you have to go, "OK, well, I might die. OK, what does that mean? And if I do die, what do I want to do?" I think that I felt like there was a lot of grace during that time for me, and it was really beautiful. I was really happy that I had that kind of structure in my life to fall back on. And I ran towards it." In turn, illness provided an opportunity "to go deeper into what [she] already had." Several African American women thanked the God who had watched over them. "I'm alive! I'm walking around," one exclaimed. "I praise God for that." Annie Briggs said, "It was nothing but the grace of Him and His garment is the reason I'm still here."

Gratitude for the support that had surrounded them during treatment also encouraged women to reach out to others in new ways. "Cancer gave me time to think, you know, what do I really find the most important in my life?" one survivor stated. "And it wasn't the things in my life; I realized it was the people. And I had sort of always kept them over here, thinking I can do anything by myself. And I realized I couldn't. And that was transformative for me, to let people in. It was the first time in my life that I ever allowed anybody to help me. So I learned a lot." Another woman also had prided herself on giving rather than receiving care. Asked to specify the "best thing" that resulted from her cancer experience, she responded, "Realizing the support that I have and the joy of relationships. I really didn't know how to be as loving or as accepting. It was hard for me to take love in. I could give it better than I could take it." A third woman began to devote greater attention to meal preparation:

> I turned fifty, and I thought, "This is ridiculous. You're fifty and you can't cook? What's going on here? You're a capable person. You should be able to have people over and make a meal." I think I was being shocked and appalled that I had gotten to this point in my life and that I didn't really cook. . . . I'm not somebody that thinks about food a lot, and I could really eat the same thing every day. But I live with other people who have different feelings about that. I would say to my kids, "Well, we just had dinner yesterday. Do we have to have dinner again?" [Laughs] And I don't cook every day, but I mean for Thanksgiving I make some dishes. That's a definite change. People who know me are just shocked. . . . I've come of age during a period of time when you just rejected domestic virtues. So I never wanted that kind of identification. My identity is formed enough that it doesn't matter. I'm also older and wiser, and times have changed. This was an effect of having had cancer. When I was ill, I had a small circle of people that knew. I got so much from people. It was truly moving how people were there for me and my family. I've always been someone who felt this way, but it was so underscored that just really, what life is about is human connection. I really witnessed firsthand the power of kindness, and it really changed me. Not that I wasn't a kind person before, not that I didn't value relationships, but it was really a profound experience being a recipient of that. Ever since I've had cancer, really all I've wanted is to give back. I think cooking is part of that, giving food to people. And not just making it slapdash, but making an effort and putting something of myself into it. It's more of an offering that way.

Like many African American women, Ida Jaffe framed her trans-formation in religious terms: before cancer, "my life was on a fast track of shopping and me. It was all about me. I never took the time to call people. I wasn't a caller, just talk to people to see how they are or what's happening in your life. I was never that kind of person. It was all about me." But "God saw something in me that he wanted to change. He had been telling me to change, and I wouldn't change, and so he gave me time to think about it and make a change in my life and make it for a good thing. Now I'm able to see and help other people, but before this I wouldn't have taken the time of day." When her mother fell ill, Ida was able to help:

> I think this was one of the greatest things that came out of me hav-ing cancer. My mother was diagnosed with cancer four years after me. I was able to mentor my mother. Even saying it was my mother, I don't think I would have taken the love, time, and care to actu-ally take care of her. I moved back to Ohio and lived there for two years to take care of my mother. She was diagnosed at ninety years old. I took care of her for two years, and I mentored her through her cancer, and she eventually passed away. I lived there and took care of her. Just to be with her every day and tell her, "This is what you'll go through, and this is what you'll experience." She didn't have the chemo and radiation because she herself decided against it. She was happy. She was OK with where she was. The cancer had metastasized throughout her body, but yet she was a happy person I think because I was there to say I'd been there, done that: "These are some of the things that you'll go through." Had I not had can-cer I couldn't have done that. I tell people that your mother is your trainer through all of your life. You learn the most important lessons from your mother. I had the joy of my mother birthing me, leading me through life, but in the last stages of life, my mother taught me how to die gracefully. That was the biggest lesson for me.

But some survivors moved in the opposite direction.[7] One, for example, said personal growth involved learning to separate from friends and family: "I feel that I've been sensitive to their needs much too long." Greater self-confidence gave another woman the courage to stand up for herself for the first time: "The women at work kind of think it's funny that I can be such a witch. You know, when they have a problem, 'Give it to her because she'll handle it!' They don't want to bring up anything. To me, it's like I have no problem! I'll deal with it! You have a problem, 'Give it to me. I'll go talk to them.' I'm a lot bolder since I went through chemo. The fight's in me." Her newly discovered inner strength found expression at home as well as at work: "I used to be a very shy person. [My son] had a friend that would come over and take all of his toys away from him. And I was never a mom that would say, 'Don't do that to my son.' Now if anybody hurt my kids they better stand back or run because I'm not going to tolerate it anymore. I became bolder in that I'm going to take care of what I have while I'm alive." It is difficult to avoid reading her son's toys as a metaphor for her own life, which she had learned to value in a new way.

When we asked another survivor how her outlook had altered, she answered, "Before, I was more guarded about hurting people's feelings, so I wouldn't say things. Now I really don't care as much." She described the "best thing" to come from her experience this way: "I don't sit up and worry about how people think about me." Another interviewee illustrated her "new sense of who I am and my place in the world" with this example:

> One of the women who was in the support group that I had formed was really hard to get along with. At some point she got her nose out of joint about something, and I can't remember what the issue was. She said, "I'm not going to come unless X, Y, and Z are going to happen." I said, "You know what, I'm not going to deal with this. Life is too short. If she wants to come, fine, but I'm not going to change my personality or the way I go about my life to try to pussyfoot around her. Tough, she needs to grow up and get with it. If she doesn't want to come, then OK." There were certain things she didn't want to discuss or something, and I just said, "I'm out of here. I'll go. You guys can go and meet on your own, but I'm out of here. I'll go. You guys can meet on your own, but I'm not going to put up with this." I told her, and she really was upset and never

came again. . . . So I find that I have to go ahead and I say what I say. I try not to hurt people's feelings, but there's this overwhelming mantra of "life is short" that I didn't have before.

Tessa McKnight had one piece of advice for women with breast cancer: "Forget about what people want from you or need from you." Excessive responsiveness to others could even harm: "One of the things they say about breast cancer psychologically is that it's women who were always like 'the breast is like milk, giving.' It's women who were always giving, giving, giving, and if that's true, . . . then it's the time to not be doing that. Get a different disease."

Change also altered women's sense of time. "It was such a pleasure," Marge noted, "those little moments" when friends brought food after chemotherapy. With her work life suspended, time slowed down, and "an hour became so interesting." An ex-nurse viewed herself as "more strongly in the here and now" because cognitive deficits prevented her from planning for the future or remembering the past: "I can't do this thing that I used to do where I could kind of think about tomorrow. I don't know how to describe what I used to do. It was like a thinking-process thing, get out of the here and now and plan or conceptualize. My experience of living is much more immediate, and I can't seem to do anything else. That seems to me related to the memory thing. I hold on to the moment because I don't have the ability to hold on to memories." Although she described herself as "trapped," she emphasized that her new orientation was "not a bad thing."[8]

Many more women explained the heightened intensity of the present as a response to their new awareness of the uncertainty of the future. "Before, I think I was more focusing on long-term goals," one remarked. "What happens is you run through the present, and you don't really see it, and suddenly it's past. I don't think I do that now. Even if I'm going through it, I'm watching myself go through it. I mean I'm actually in there." Another woman delighted in sights and sounds once taken for granted. "Everything changed," she reflected, "like listening. I've been hearing my kids talk all their lives, but right after that, I heard my baby—it was like different—the way she said 'Mama.' Just the way she said 'Mama,' I had never heard it before this way. And like when I walk now, I look at the trees, the flowers, the grass, the cracks in the ground. I look at everything now. It's like I'm taking it all in. Everything! I don't wanna miss nothing. I really don't." The transience of life made Annie Briggs want to "capture every moment": "whether it'd be walking on the beach, window shopping, talking to an elder, a kid making you laugh, seeing birds fly, running water, going to get a bag of potato chips from the store and enjoying them like I've never enjoyed them before." Yet another survivor compared herself to a woman overheard while getting a pedicure:

> She was complaining how when she turned fifty, "I'm going to bed, and I'm going to sleep." I was thinking, "You stupid woman. Don't let a major life-threatening illness make you appreciate that you are alive at fifty." Because that's what it's done. My fiftieth birthday is coming up, and my daughter and my mother are coming up. They're throwing me a huge party. They're not too happy with all the people I invited, but I'm here, I'm alive, and I'm celebrating. . . . It took this to make me understand how important it is to be getting older. I didn't understand it before, and that part is real positive. I would love to learn how to be a speaker to go around to tell women not to wait to let something that almost kills you teach you to appreciate life. I mean, life is something to be cherished. It's a gift, and it can be taken away at any time.

Postponing gratification no longer made sense. One survivor said, "If I see something I want and I have the money—I might not have the money, but if I can get it, I'm getting it! I was watching a show on TV and there was this young girl, and she said that when she got diagnosed and got through treatment, she wanted a Corvette. I don't have the money to go buy a Corvette, but if I see something I want, I'm gonna get it, if it's at all in my ability, because I wanna be able to enjoy life because you just don't know if you're gonna be here tomorrow." Another survivor seized a nonmaterial pleasure: "When I was in the mayor's office, we had Christmas carolers in the office, and I had something I was supposed to do, and I was like, 'The hell with it. I'm going to listen to the Christmas carolers because I might never hear them again.'"

Although pain and fatigue caused some women to forgo trips they had planned, others embarked on travels they previously never would have contemplated. "Life is short," one woman remarked.

> You don't know what's coming your way, and I never would travel, but I went to New York the year after I had my surgery. I probably would never have gone. I really don't like to travel, but since I had my treatment and everything, I've gone to visit friends in New York and Connecticut and Oregon. I get up and go. I've never been to the East Coast, and I was like, "This is beautiful. This is so nice." This friend said, "Oh, we're going to New York," and I said, "Of course." She said, "We're going in June," and I said, "Absolutely." She sent me these postcards, and I thought, "She's got to be kidding. I'm not really going." And she bought the tickets, and I said, "You bought the tickets?" So I said, "Oh gosh, I guess I'm going." So I went, and I'm so glad that she did that. I would have never gone. I would have never seen New York.

Two women made more ambitious plans. "I hate to fly," one said, "but my daughter and I went over to Italy. I took the Dramamine, got on the plane, and tried it. So we're doing things that I didn't think I would have tried." The voyage of the second woman was still in the future: "I don't put off things now. For example, my sister turned fifty two weeks ago, and I said, 'Where would you like to go?' and she said, 'Outside of the United States.' She said, 'I have always wanted to go there.' So I'm taking my sister to Paris for her fiftieth birthday. And I will never again hesitate: 'Should I get together with that person? Should I take my trip now or should I wait?'"

Women also tried to fulfill long-standing vocational ambitions. An elementary school teacher was well aware of the costs of returning to school to become an educational administrator. She would be forced to forfeit "all recreation and family life for two years and every bit of summer travel" that she would "usually do for fun." Because she had been diagnosed with metastatic cancer, she realized she could not "expect to survive forever." And her general practitioner had cautioned her against embarking on a "high-stress career." Nevertheless, a few months before we interviewed her, she had enrolled in classes. "I finally decided it is way more high stress not doing what you want to do, so I went back to school. It sounds very stupid, but I wanted to live my life to the fullest, and to me this part is a means to an end."

If cancer encouraged women to open themselves to new possibilities, it also led them to drop old preoccupations. Two African Americans lost interest in hair styling. "It's like I was relieved from a big burden," one commented, "a freedom from hair." The other said, "One of the things that I have recognized from the illness is that in African Americans, we have this odd thing about hair, and I have learned to enjoy my hair for what it is. I don't have to have it straight; I don't have to have it one certain way. To me, going to the hair shop and spending hours at a time is a waste of time. My life means more to me now than to be sitting in a hairdresser shop all day long."

Other survivors relinquished vocational ambitions. Whereas the teacher embarked on a career as an educational administrator, Marge reconsidered her own fast-track career. Ida Jaffe noted that reordered priorities as well as cognitive difficulties explained her decision to quit her administrative position: "After cancer you realize that there is more to life than things, for instance, like new cars, shopping, clothes, or rings, and the biggest or best watch, the biggest diamond ring or the biggest trip."

Women who withdrew from the workforce often found other activities that nourished them. A former nurse rediscovered the joy of music: "I'm not sitting in the corner crying. I have too many other things going on in my life right now. For instance for this semester I took an arranging class because I've always wanted to learn how to arrange music. I've also taken all my harmony classes. Last night they performed a song I wrote and arranged. That's pretty significant for me." Another ex-nurse viewed art as a partial compensation for career loss: "One of the thrills of nursing, as in any profession, is helping people. It's the connection with the higher power and higher energy, and when you're good in making a difference in people's lives, [it's] bringing heaven to earth. It's a powerful addictive thing, and it's hard to let go of. When you can't do it anymore you know that you are in danger." When she realized she could no longer continue in her profession, she asked herself, "How am I going to be defined as a Christian?" Her answer: "I think the art is it."

Another way women were able to infuse their cancer experience with meaning was by engaging in social action. There were ample opportunities for doing so. Founded in 1991, the National Breast Cancer Coalition consists of hundreds of member organizations and tens of thousands of individuals, who seek increased funding for breast cancer research, expanded access to breast cancer screening, diagnosis, and treatment, and greater involvement of patients and survivors in establishing the policy agenda for fighting the disease.[9] Several women in this study traveled to Sacramento or Washington, D.C., to lobby legislators. Many also worked at the local level. One viewed herself as "turning a bad experience into something good" by serving on the survivors advisory board at the hospital where she received treatment. Another helped to obtain services for others that had not been available for her. Her group of volunteers successfully campaigned to provide a breast cancer counselor at a hospital's West L.A. facility and to insert messages about mammograms on the answering machine.

Educational efforts represent another form of activism. Having learned from her support group how to communicate with her doctor, Marsha Dixler now had a mission to teach others:

> I try to tell them, "You take control. Usually when you go see a doctor a lot of times they have extra copies. You can get a copy of your blood report, look at it for yourself, see what they tell you the baseline is. And then once you see the baseline, then you get the report the next time, you look at it for yourself." And just go like that. I try to tell them I am very, very plain. "I'm from a city that's about that big in Arkansas. If you blink your eye you would definitely miss it. So it's not that I'm so great or I speak up, but if I can do it, plain Jane, you can too. You have a step up above me. You grew up in California. I grew up in Arkansas."

One highly educated woman taught her doctor about the special difficulties of survivors after cancer: "I'm someone who is very comfortable talking to doctors and asking questions and telling them what's going on," she explained. "I would go in, and I would say, 'Steve, I'm having memory problems.'" Because other women were less forthcoming, he needed to take the initiative:

> I said, "I'll come in and tell you, but there is probably somebody in the next room, and that's your job." I said, "Look, we're not just blood counts. I can be an advocate for myself, but I know it's hard for a lot of people, and my heart goes out to them. And I really think it's the responsibility of the physician to acknowledge or inform people that you might have a memory [problem]." He was very receptive. He said, "You're right. Sometimes I'm so backed up and so unconscious, and I'm running late and people are waiting." And I can understand that, and there is that pressure, but I said, "You know what? It's going to be an extra fifteen minutes, but if people know that when you come in the room they're not going to feel rushed and that you're going to sit and talk to them, they're not going to care that much. They know that they're going to get that kind of care, or that's why you're backed up. People come into these rooms and they are frightened. They've been told that they've had cancer, and basically they want to know if they are going to live. So that's what you're dealing with, and some people are too frightened to ask questions." He was very responsive.

Women explained their commitment to work for change in various ways. Three African Americans asserted that God had selected them to act on behalf of others. Pat Garland, for example, was able to find a reason for the many miseries she had confronted since treatment ended: "I know that every breast cancer survivor's story is not as bad as mine, which also makes me angry. Who picked me? But I figure that God picked me because I'm vocal. So that there is some woman over there in the corner that would like to be able to articulate, and she can't. But I can. I can speak for her. So I kind of look at that as why God chose me to have so many problems."

Racial injustice galvanized two other African Americans. "Black women are dying at a higher rate than white women," Ida Jaffe said, "because we're diagnosed later. I don't think we're getting the same treatment. . . . I was one of the lucky ones about the top-quality treatment. Some black women don't have the insurance in support of the treatment that you can get. That's an issue that's falling by the wayside." A second woman declared, "When you see the TV commercials, you always see a white woman up there. A group of white women with breast cancer. They don't usually share. This is why we thought it was a white woman's disease. It's because they had the commercials; on it was always a picture of a white woman. In the books and everything, always white. But we have to change that."[10]

Both black and white women pointed to other motives as well. One survivor noted that the "strength" she had gained from cancer and its aftermath enabled her to give speeches and meet legislators, activities she previously would not have considered. Another woman said, "I want to give back because someone gave to me when I was going through it, because I didn't know what to expect, you know? If you said, 'What is chemotherapy? What is radiation? What do you need to anticipate?' I had no idea. But someone was there to talk to me, and that made me feel good. So I'm going to do something. So that's what I do. I volunteer for the American Cancer Society. That helps me. It makes me feel good to do that." A third woman hoped to give other survivors the kind of help that had been unavailable to her: "It's more than a full-time job when you're done with treatment, because now you have all these symptoms left over and everyone goes, 'You're doing good. You're going to live.' But you don't know what to do or where to go, and there is no one to help you. I don't want other people to have to go through this."

Finally, a woman defined her activism as an outgrowth of her heightened awareness of the needs of others. Understanding the vulnerability she shared with all other victims of breast cancer, she began to see the inequities in the health care system more clearly than ever before:

> I'm grateful that I have access to the care that I have and the medical insurance that enables me to have the treatments and be able to afford it. I think about the people that don't have the same privilege. That's one thing that has changed. I actively think about people that don't have access to the medical care and assistance that I do, and it's terribly disturbing to me. Theoretically I would always

be disturbed about that, but it's something that I really think about within the course of my day, in a way that I didn't before. Just last week I had to have those tests. They are incredibly costly, but I have really good health insurance, and I think about somebody else who doesn't and so, what does that mean? Does that mean that they don't go for follow-up? Does that mean that the doctors are more dismissive? I'm sure there are any number of scenarios, and I think that I have become much more sensitive to those issues, actively sensitive than I was before. It's just such a gross inequity, and I feel really fortunate. It's not that I want to give up my place, but I really see the ramifications of not having that privilege. Having experienced illness and understanding it in a real term what that means, whether in terms of treatment or having access to the medications that you need afterwards, the prescription drugs. I have a prescription drug plan, so I pay and it has gone up, but I'm still only paying twenty-five dollars for drugs that I know cost hundreds of dollars. And that's terrible. That's criminal. I see my attitude toward the health care system has really changed. Again, I think I had the same attitude before, but it's much more pronounced because I understand it in a different way, and I really feel ethically obligated to do what I can to change it. I contact my senators now. I've always been politically aware, but for a number of reasons, I'm more politically active than I was before.

This quotation bears a striking similarity to a famous passage by Albert Schweitzer. Drawing on the intimate knowledge of suffering he gained both as a missionary in Africa and as a prisoner with a serious illness during World War I, Schweitzer wrote, "Whoever among us has learned through personal experience what pain and anxiety really are must help to ensure that those out there who are in physical need obtain the same help that once came to him. He no longer belongs to himself alone; he has become the brother of all who suffer. It is this 'brotherhood of those who bear the mark of pain' that demands humane medical services."[11] Viewing herself as part of a sisterhood of breast cancer patients and survivors, this woman felt "ethically obligated" to fight for expanded health care access.

Beyond the Cure

We argued at the beginning of this book that the cultural denial of both death and disability rendered breast cancer virtually invisible throughout much of its history. In the early twentieth century, however, the American Cancer Society launched a massive campaign to shatter that "conspiracy of silence."[12] Substituting positive for negative images, widely distributed films, lectures, posters, magazine articles, and personal memoirs asserted that anyone who followed the reigning medical advice could not only survive the disease but also regain good health and live normally. The mainstream breast cancer movement today is even more upbeat. Now women can not just survive the disease; they can go on to have even better, more profound existences. Endowing the disease with far greater visibility than ever before, various organizations sponsor highly publicized events where survivors display and celebrate their renewed physical prowess.

This chapter demonstrates that women who work within that movement often tell stories sharply at odds with its Panglossian view. No longer avoiding the inevitable frailty of the human condition, they seek to live more fully within vulnerable bodies. Marge Barlow made a virtue of uncertainty, embracing the possibility that her career would "unfold" in a different way from the one she originally charted. In another case, illness heightened a sense of responsibility for others. And many women found new appreciation for the minutiae of life once taken for granted.

Survivors with lingering health problems are hardly unique in using the confrontation with mortality as an opportunity for inner growth. As we have seen, breast cancer narratives commonly emphasize the spiritual awakenings that enrich the survivors' lives. Nevertheless, women who fail to recover completely may have an especially intense need to seek meaning in their experiences and reorient their lives. Few women we interviewed could view breast cancer as a brief interruption. As a result, old ways of being seemed especially inappropriate.

Conclusion

"THE HEALING PROCESS begins," according to physician Rita Charon, "when patients tell of symptoms or even fears of illness—first to themselves, then to loved ones, and finally to health professionals."[1] In the stories we heard, that process was badly flawed. The primary response of "loved ones" was to urge the women to ignore their symptoms and move on with their lives. Many survivors went from doctor to doctor, seeking one who would validate their experiences and offer relief. Even problems that severely constrained central life activities were dismissed as trivial or nonexistent. The absence of medical certification impeded efforts to convince family and friends that the problems were "real." Some women began to doubt their own feelings.

Much has changed in the few years since those events occurred. As a proliferating literature continues to document the myriad problems besetting the nation's 2.5 million breast cancer survivors, the news increasingly captures public attention. The front page of the April 29, 2007, *New York Times* announces, "Chemotherapy Fog Is No Longer Ignored as Illusion."[2] Recent advice books about life after treatment include tips about managing chemobrain and fatigue.[3] Survivors have begun to share experiences of symptoms online. Internet sites provide fact sheets women can download to convince skeptical doctors the problems are real.

Anecdotal evidence suggests that many doctors no longer need to be convinced. A growing number now warn about long-term side effects before administering treatment and acknowledge those that occur. Another response has been the development of methods to tailor drugs to individual patients. Two "gene classifier tests" can now be performed on tumors, allowing for "more selective and less toxic treatments."[4] A large randomized trial called TAILORx has been inaugurated to determine which women with intermediate risk of recurrence would benefit from chemotherapy.[5]

Growing recognition of the problems experienced after various forms of cancer treatment has led to the establishment of special medical programs for survivors. The Lance Armstrong Foundation recently funded five comprehensive cancer centers to establish "Livestrong Survivorship Centers of Excellence." The UCLA center, directed by Dr. Patricia Ganz, conducts research into the most critical issues confronting survivors, coordinates their care in the community, and pioneers new forms of service delivery.[6]

But fixing the "healing process" will take more fundamental reforms as well. The key complaint of our interviewees was that doctors failed to listen to them. We hear similar complaints everywhere— and not only from patients. Dr. Jerome Groopman opens his widely acclaimed new book, *How Doctors Think*, with an account of Anne Dodge, who had consulted nearly thirty doctors for her increasingly debilitating gastrointestinal symptoms. She received the diagnosis of anorexia and irritable bowel syndrome but continued to waste away. Severely malnourished after fifteen years, Anne found a doctor who did something different. He observed her manner, listened to her story, and diagnosed celiac disease, a serious autoimmune disorder. Groopman insists that doctors must pay more attention to patient reports and resist the temptation to dismiss poorly understood symptoms as psychosomatic.[7]

Some posttreatment symptoms may never receive medical confirmation. As physician and medical historian Robert Aronowitz writes, "a great deal of individual suffering . . . must necessarily be accepted as idiosyncratic." Aronowitz urges both doctors and patients to acknowledge "the limits of current medical knowledge and the multifaceted, contingent nature of the way we experience pain, fatigue, and other aspects of our bodily and emotional awareness."[8] Although medical researchers increasingly document the serious consequences of breast cancer therapy, many of the symptoms our interviewees reported continue to defy medical understanding. Some have not (yet) been identified as treatment aftereffects. And the etiology of much fatigue, cognitive impairment, and pain was often murky in individual cases. Survivors need to be able to convince others of the reality of their suffering even when there is no clear causal nexus.

Many observers fault medical training for the inability of doctors to listen more closely to their patients. Watching the new crop of students and residents in his hospital "eye their algorithms and then invoke statistics from recent studies," Groopman concludes that "the next generation of doctors was being conditioned to function like a well-programmed computer that operates within a strict binary framework."[9] The rise of medical humanities programs thus represents a promising development.[10] By 2004, 88 of 125 U.S. medical schools surveyed by the American Association of Medical Colleges offered classes in the human dimensions of care, including treating patients as whole people, respecting their cultural values, and responding empathetically to their pain and suffering.[11] But such courses never will constitute more than a tiny fraction of medical-school curricula. And the growing power of the insurance industry to shape medical practice undermines the lessons they teach. As several survivors reminded us, a major reason doctors fail to take the time to listen is that insurance companies increasingly demand a frenetic work pace. At the most basic level, this book points to the necessity of revamping a health care system in which concern for cost containment so frequently trumps care for essential human needs.

Other major reforms could improve survivors' social and economic status. Although the women in this study expressed little sense of commonality with the millions of other people experiencing physical or mental impairments, many of the perspectives of the rapidly growing disability movement are extremely relevant to the stories we heard. A key tenet of the movement is that the problems encountered by people with disabilities stem at least as much from social arrangements as from individual impairments.[12] Two features of contemporary employment present special impediments for survivors with limited energy: the accelerated pace of work and the long work week.[13] One woman arrived home exhausted whenever she was "timed and rushed." The major obstacle a nurse faced was not the many hours her hospital demanded but, rather, the way they were organized. Too weak to render care for twelve hours at a stretch, she was forced to retire.

The disability movement also challenges the widespread belief in the inevitability of individual progress.[14] Most women we interviewed immediately understood that a breast cancer diagnosis meant that the threat of a recurrence would never disappear. Virtually none of the women, however, had anticipated that recovery from acute treatment side effects might not follow a linear pattern. Living in a society that expects everyone to overcome any adversity, many survivors felt intense shame about lingering health problems. Consequently, some neither asserted their rights to accommodations at work nor demanded adequate support at home. Expectations of cure also produce a deep current of suspicion about chronic problems. Our interviewees may have been right to fear that many close relatives and employers would view talk of persistent side effects as signs of malingering. In order to honor breast cancer survivors' stories, we should work to dismantle both the social structures and cultural ideals that encumber the lives of all disabled people.

Epilogue

BECAUSE POSTTREATMENT SYMPTOMS are long-term, we wanted to know how they change over time. In the spring of 2007, approximately five years after the initial interviews, we spoke again to ten of the eleven women who figure most prominently in this book. (The remaining woman could not be contacted.) Only one survivor had experienced a recurrence of breast cancer. We also were happy to learn that in some cases the symptoms had improved. Several women, however, continue to struggle with serious health problems.

Marge Barlow

Marge Barlow's career dilemma resolved "accidentally." The year after we first spoke with her, a large state university "recruited" her and then offered her a position as an assistant professor. "I did not feel like I could say no to an academic appointment that sort of fell in my lap," she said. "I also thought it would be a nice fresh start to my life."

But her ambition remains modest: "In truth, one reason I took this job was because it is a research university but a low-ranked department, where the demands are not high." She finally finished her dissertation and then converted it into the book she will need for tenure; a prestigious university press will publish it. Nevertheless, she insisted, "The drive is simply gone for the career. It is hard for me to maintain interest in working. Part of this is middle-age angst, I think (I'll be fifty-three this week), but another part of it involves a shift for me thinking more about mortality and prioritizing what is important. This is the residue that resonates most clearly for me with that 'cancer space' I enjoyed so much."

Although Marge's memory lapses occur far less frequently than before, they continue to embarrass her: "When my brain simply checks out, like in the middle of class, it is unnerving, and I have to make a joke about it." Her mother recently told Marge, "with regret and compassion," that it was clear she still had not regained her former sharpness and energy.

Annie Briggs

Annie Briggs has had eight breast cancer recurrences during the past ten years and recently learned that the disease has spread to her liver. Because she has not worked since her original diagnosis, paying rent has been a "struggle." She remains estranged from her family and finds any contact "painful." Her faith sustains her: "You just can't foresee tomorrow. My cup runneth over, and I will create a monument before I leave this earth. He said He would never forsake me, and now I welcome this disease and everything that is transpiring. I thank Him for what He has done and what He will do."

Marsha Dixler

Since her retirement, Marsha Dixler has been able to devote even more time than before to the breast cancer movement. A member of the National Breast Cancer Coalition, she frequently lobbies legislators in Sacramento and Washington, D.C., to increase access to care for low-income women. She also remains committed to teaching others the advocacy skills she honed so successfully herself. One way is by working as a "patient navigator" at a local hospital. "People get nervous with doctors. I ask, 'What do you want to know? Let's write it in the form of a question. You are paying the doctor, and if he don't know your answer, he needs to find it and get back to you.'" In addition, she works with "Each One Teach One," a project of the Women of Color Breast Cancer Survivors Support Group, preaching the importance of early detection. Her primary responsibility is to phone women who have participated in the program "to verify that they are doing what we've taught. But many African Americans don't! I call and tell them who I am, not soliciting, just following up my part of the promise. 'Are you doing your part?' They laugh and thank me for reminding them. I say, 'I'm going to give you a chance, but I am not going to go away.' I'll call back in a couple of months, and I will call to see if they have their mammograms. I am trying to encourage them to take control of their own life."

Although Marsha's symptoms have abated, she faces a new challenge. Having been advised to have her ovaries and fallopian tubes removed, she has decided to undergo a complete hysterectomy. One reason is that she already has gone through menopause: "The chemo did that." In addition, her family history suggests she cannot afford to take chances. A sister has had breast cancer; three first cousins have died of the disease; and an aunt has died of ovarian cancer. But Marsha also feels competent to deal with whatever befalls her. Having worked in the breast cancer movement for years, she has the resources she would need to remain actively involved in her care.

Pat Garland

Pat Garland remains unemployed as a result of her various disabilities. Two of her major posttreatment symptoms (joint pain and neuropathy) have become worse. The chemobrain, however, has improved since Pat ceased responding with "anger and fear." "Once I could accept that it wasn't just me, I started helping myself with tricks. I became a writer from hell, with memos everywhere. I used my cell phone and calendar to help me remember things that should not be forgotten." Pat withdrew from the breast cancer movement after realizing that she "used it as an escape": "Eventually I had to stop and pay attention to me."

The responses of doctors to Pat's new health problems have helped to stoke her rage at the health care system. When she developed severe bursitis in her hips and a pinched nerve in her neck two years ago, her doctors assumed the cancer had returned and thus refused to refer her to appropriate specialists for many months.

Ida Jaffe

Ida Jaffe described herself as "very well, very healthy." Part of the credit, she believes, goes to her family: "I have a great husband." Both daughters are doing well, one a nurse and the other in elder home care. She also attributes her recovery to her hobbies. Yoga has made the joint pain "more manageable." Line dancing helps improve her memory.

She remains involved in breast cancer activities, participating in the American Cancer Society Reach to Recovery Program and attending the meetings of five support groups (Women of Color, Women of Essence, Sisters, My Friend, and You Are Not Alone). Because she has a "large network," she is able to provide a great deal of informal help to patients: "People call me and ask, 'Hey, can you take this person to their first visit? Here's someone who is going to chemo—can you drive back and forth?'" The various support groups also keep her "abreast of everything that is going on—new drugs and treatments and protocols."

Rose Jensen

Rose Jensen's family and employment situation remains largely unchanged. Although her older daughter has left home to attend Occidental College, Rose and her other child still live with Rose's mother. Having quit her "high-powered" engineering job to cope with her many posttreatment side effects, Rose continues to work as an office manager at a local university. The cognitive impairment has not improved: "My mind was a steel trap; now I literally have problems remembering where my keys are."

Rose's long struggle with cancer and its aftermath appear to have influenced her college-age daughter, who recently declared herself "premed" and hopes to become an oncologist. Both children worry how Rose will fare when the younger one leaves home in two years, and they encourage their mother to stop focusing on them and try to start doing things for herself. That, she considers, a "scary notion." Her social life remains extremely restricted, and she is reluctant even to contemplate dating again. One reason is her libido, which was "nuked to ground zero" and has never returned. The other is her medical history. So many men her age have lost a wife or significant other to cancer that any reference to that diagnosis is "the kiss of death."

In other situations, Rose talks openly about her cancer experience and often reaches out to strangers undergoing treatment. She "approaches people without hair in the grocery store and ask[s] 'What flavor chemo?'" She misses support groups, which she stopped attending a few years after treatment ended: "Places don't want you when you're cured." But she thinks "it would be nice" to gather every month or so with other survivors, not "in a classroom or conference room" but, rather, to take a walk at the beach and "just chat" about the many issues they face in common.

Tessa McKnight

Seven years after her last chemotherapy appointment, Tessa McKnight is thriving. She still loves her work in her flower shop, feels "great," and can barely remember her posttreatment symptoms. Although she has regular biannual checkups with her oncologist and participates in breast cancer fund-raising walks, the disease is no longer a major part of her life.

Leanne Thomas

Leanne Thomas continues to experience several posttreatment symptoms, including memory loss, insomnia, and depression, and to rely heavily on both alternative remedies and self-help measures. She regularly exercises, meditates, does yoga ("not as often as I should, but I am a big believer") and watches her diet carefully, "staying away from red meat and eating fish and chicken and vegetables." No longer seeing her therapist, she attends a weekly depression group organized by her health plan.

She continues to be an enthusiastic member of the Sisters support group: "It's nice to understand that you're not the only person going through this and that. You share, and people say, 'I feel that way.' That makes me feel better because I thought there was something wrong with me, but I'm not the only one." In addition, she "gives back" by doing outreach for the American Cancer Society, speaking "to people who have been diagnosed and answering their questions." She does similar work at a local hospital, where, like Marsha Dixler, she serves as a "navigator" for cancer patients. "You can let people know what to anticipate, and they really appreciate it. They have never gone through this, and you have."

Jean Trawick

Since her diagnosis with Crohn's disease three years ago, Jean Trawick's confusion about the genesis of her enduring fatigue has increased. Is the cause cancer treatment, advancing age, this new health problem, or a combination of all three? The sequelae of her reconstruction surgery also continue to trouble her. The implant has shrunk to such an extent that she resorts to a prosthesis. Because radiation damaged her skin, she would need very extensive surgery to correct the problem and is unwilling to contemplate that.

She remains highly critical of traditional medical care. Despite her ability to "work the system," she has trouble gaining access to doctors. As a result, she continues to rely on a nurse practitioner in a San Francisco wellness center as her primary provider. The mainstream health care system, Jean concludes, is "good for crises, but for chronic illness it is a mess."

Jean eventually relinquished her ambition to enter educational administration. Having retired from teaching, she now devotes much of her time to photography; a portrait shot during a trip to Hawaii recently won a prize.

Nina Worth

Nina Worth has wonderful news: the menopause she experienced during chemotherapy proved temporary, and three years after it ended, she gave birth to a son, who is about to celebrate his third birthday. Her chemobrain also disappeared, and although she still suffers from bone pain, it is less intense than before. She remains "happily married" to the man she met during treatment and continues to raise funds for cancer research.

Appendix

ALTHOUGH THIS BOOK is a joint product, the two authors worked independently. Saskia obtained the grant, designed the questionnaire, and led the research team. She then was forced to turn her attention to other projects. Emily thus did the analysis and writing on her own.

Because the goal was not to document the existence of symptoms but, rather, to understand how people lived with and made sense of them, Saskia used a qualitative methodology. Her research team included an anthropologist, an oncology nurse, a doctoral candidate in psychology, and a master's candidate in public health.

Breast cancer survivors were eligible if they were at least one year beyond completion of adjuvant radiation and/or chemotherapy (some were continuing with Tamoxifen, a hormonal therapy). Recruitment occurred through the distribution and posting of flyers at a variety of locations, including cancer wellness centers, physicians' offices, places of worship, prosthetic supply stores, and support-group meeting sites. Respondents to the flyers were prescreened by phone for basic demographic information. Because participants self-nominated, our sample may have been somewhat skewed. Whenever possible, however, we compare our results to those of quantitiave studies.

Saskia initially planned to study three groups of women: African Americans, Hispanics, and whites. She had no difficulty recruiting whites and African Americans. The latter group, in particular, was extremely supportive of the endeavor; African American support-group leaders throughout Los Angeles posted the flyers and announced information about the study during their gatherings. All but two of the African American women in this study were interviewed by a fieldworker from Kenya. She developed such an extraordinary rapport with the respondents that many referred friends from their churches, neighborhoods, or support groups to our project. It is our speculation that beyond the charisma of that fieldworker, the project appealed to African American survivors beacuse it provided them with a venue to voice their dissatisfaction with the health care system.

Saskia also hired two half-time, bilingual Latina fieldworkers to recruit Hispanic respondents. All the recruitment materials were translated into Spanish and back-translated for accuracy. In addition to the recruitment venues used for our other respondents, the fieldworkers went into numerous local settings, including neighborhood markets, free clinics, and community hopitals. Nevertheless, no Latina respondent joined our study. One explanation might involve access to health care. Latinas who are poor and/or undocumented may be more likely to seek treatment at later stages; as a result, the posttreatment symptoms might not be considered either unusual or especially troubling. Other explanations may lie in cultural differences. After the fact, a colleague who studies Latino families suggested that we might have had more success if we had tried to recruit the Latinas through their husbands, because women would not participate in a research study without the express consent of their male partners. It also is possible that many Latinas perceived the posttreatment symptoms as simply one more burden to bear or the "will of God." Nevertheless, we remain convinced that future studies should make every effort to include Latinas as well as Asian populations.

Early in the fall of 2002, Saskia conducted four focus groups (two with African Americans and two with whites) to collect preliminary data and help refine the questionnaire. Throughout the following ten months, she and her team conducted in-depth interviews, lasting between one and three hours, with seventy-four women, twenty-two of whom had participated in the focus groups. Questions elicited data about medical background, treatment experience, the nature of posttreatment symptoms, reactions from both medical personnel and friends and family, self-management of symptoms, and evolving perceptions of self. All interviews were recorded, transcribed, and coded.

The following tables present demographic information about the seventy-four women:

DEMOGRAPHICS OF RESPONDENTS

Age	N	%
30–39	2	2.80
40–49	16	22.54
50–50	30	42.50
60–69	15	21.13
70–79	6	8.45
80–89	2	2.82
Missing	1	

Marital Status	N	%
Married	27	38.57
Divorced	22	31.43
Separated	4	5.71
Widowed	7	10.00
Single	7	10.00
Unmarried, living with partner	2	2.86
Other	1	1.43
Missing	2	

Number of Children	N	%
0	14	20.59
1	10	14.71
2	25	36.76
3	12	17.65
4	3	4.41
5	4	5.88
6	0	0.00
Missing	4	

Education Level	N	%
Less than HS	0	0.00
HS	8	11.43
Some College	26	37.14
College Graduate	18	25.71
Postgraduate Study	16	22.86
Other	2	2.86
Missing	2	

Total Family Income	N	%
Less than $10,000	6	8.96
$10,000–$14,999	4	5.97
$15,000–$19,999	6	8.96
$20,000–$24,999	3	4.48
$25,000–$29,999	3	4.48
$30,000–$34,999	2	2.99
$35,000–$39,999	7	10.45
$40,000–$49,999	9	13.43
$50,000–$59,999	2	2.99
$60,000–$74,999	11	16.42
More than $74,999	14	20.90
Missing	7	

Employment Status	N	%
Unemployed	32	45.71
Full-time	29	41.43
Part-time	9	12.86
Missing	4	

The African American and white groups were similar in terms of age, martial status, employment status, and income. The two groups differed significantly in terms of number of children (p=0.048) and education level (p=0.002).

NUMBER OF CHILDREN

African American Women	N	%
0	14	20.59
1	10	14.71
2	25	36.76
3	12	17.65
4	3	4.41
5	4	5.88
6	0	0.00
Missing	4	

White Women	N	%
0	9	27.27
1	4	12.12
2	15	45.45
3	4	12.12
4	0	0.00
5	1	3.03
6	0	0.00
Missing	5	

EDUCATION LEVEL

African American Women	N	%
Less than HS	0	0.00
HS	7	20.00
Some College	15	42.86
College Graduate	9	25.70
Postgraduate Study	3	8.57
Other	1	2.86
Missing	2	

White Women	N	%
Less than HS	0	0.00
HS	1	2.86
Some College	11	31.43
College Graduate	9	25.71
Postgraduate Study	13	37.14
Other	1	2.86
Missing	3	

Notes

Notes to the Introduction

1. Alice Stewart Trillin, "Betting Your Life," in *The Social Medicine Reader*, Vol. 1, *Patients, Doctors, and Illness*, 2nd ed., ed. Nancy M. P. King et al. (Durham, N.C.: Duke University Press, 2005), p. 33.

2. See Chris Feudtner, "A Disease in Motion: Diabetes History and the New Paradigm of Transmuted Disease," *Perspectives in Biology and Medicine*, v. 39, no. 2 (Winter 1996): 158–170.

3. For useful summaries of the patient experience of illness, see Michael Bury, "The Sociology of Chronic Illness: A Review of Research and Prospects," *Sociology of Health and Illness*, v. 13, no. 4 (1991): 451–468; Julia Lawton, "Lay Experiences of Health and Illness: Past Research and Future Agendas," *Sociology of Health and Illness*, v. 25 (Silver Anniversary Issue 2003): 23–40; Janine Pierret, "The Illness Experience: State of Knowledge and Perspectives for Research," *Sociology of Health and Illness*, v. 25 (Silver Anniversary Issue 2003): 4–22; Simon J. Williams, "Chronic Illness as Biographical Disruption or Biographical Disruption as Chronic Illness? Reflections on a Core Concept," *Sociology of Health and Illness*, v. 22, no. 1 (2000): 40–67. Studies on the aftereffects of breast cancer have grown very rapidly and are now too extensive to be listed in their entirety. For a good summary of the literature, see Institute of Medicine and National Research Council of the National Academies, *From Cancer Patient to Cancer Survivor: Lost in Transition* (Washington, D.C.: National Academies Press, 2001).

4. The appendix contains more information about the sample and methodology as well as our division of labor.

5. A recent study, relying on positron emission tomography (PET) scans, found evidence of a decline in brain functioning in breast-cancer survivors; that technology, however, was not available at the time of the interviews. See Daniel H. S. Silverman, Christine J. Dy, Steven A. Castellon, Jasmine Lai, Betty S. Pio, Laura Abraham, Kari Waddell, Laura Peterson, Michael E. Phelps, and Patricia A Ganz, "Altered Frontocortical,

Cerebellar, and Basal Ganglia Activity in Adjuvant-Treated Breast Cancer Survivors 5–10 Years after Chemotherapy," *Breast Cancer Research and Treatment,* v. 103, no. 3 (July 2007): 303–311.

6. See Kirstin K. Barker, *The Fibromyalgia Story: Medical Authority and Women's Worlds of Pain* (Philadelphia: Temple University Press, 2005); Lesley Cooper, "Myalgic Encephalomyelitis and the Medical Encounter," *Sociology of Health and Illness,* v. 19, no. 2 (1997): 186–207; Susan Greenhalgh, *Under the Medical Gaze: Facts and Fictions of Chronic Pain* (Berkeley: University of California Press, 2001); Steve Kroll-Smith and H. Hugh Floyd, *Bodies in Protest: Environmental Illness and the Struggle over Medical Knowledge* (New York: New York University Press, 1997); Norma C. Ware, "Toward a Model of Social Course in Chronic Illness: The Example of Chronic Fatigue Syndrome," *Culture, Medicine, and Psychiatry,* v. 23 (1999): 303–331; Norma C. Ware and Arthur Kleinman, "Culture and Somatic Experience: The Social Course of Illness in Neurasthenia an Chronic Fatigue Syndrome," *Psychosomatic Medicine,* v. 54 (1992): 546–560. Chronic fatigue syndrome recently has gained increased legitimacy as a result of findings from the Centers for Disease Control and Prevention that the disease may be caused by genetic factors. See David Tuller, "Chronic Fatigue No Longer Seen as 'Yuppie Flu,'" *New York Times* (July 17, 2007).

7. These accounts include Ernie Bodai and Judie Fertig Panneton, *The Breast Cancer Book of Strength and Courage: Inspiring Stories to See You through Your Journey* (Roseville, Calif.: Prima, 2002); Kathlyn Conway, *Ordinary Life: A Memoir of Illness* (New York: W. H. Freeman, 1997); Barbara Delinsky, *Uplift: Secrets from the Sisterhood of Breast Cancer Survivors* (New York: Washington Square Press, 2001); Miriam Engelberg, *Cancer Made Me a Shallower Person: A Memoir in Comics* (New York: HarperCollins, 2006); Nora Feller and Marcia Stevens Sherrill, *Portraits of Hope: Conquering Breast Cancer: 52 Inspirational Stories of Strength* (New York: Wonderland, 1998); Deborah Hobler Kahane, *No Less a Woman: Femininity, Sexuality, and Breast Cancer* (New York: Simon and Schuster, 1990); *Living on the Margins: Women Writers on Breast Cancer,* ed. Hilda Raz (New York: Persea, 1999); Jane Lazarre, *Wet Earth and Dreams: A Narrative of Grief and Recovery* (Durham, N.C.: Duke University Press, 1998); Marisa Acocella Marchetto, *Cancer Vixen: A True Story* (New York: Knopf, 2006); Peggy McCarthy and Jo An Loren, *Breast Cancer? Let Me Check My Schedule!* (Boulder, Colo.: Westview, 1997); Susan Diemert Moch, with Allan Graubard, *Breast Cancer: Twenty Women's Stories: Becoming More Alive through the Experience* (New York: MLN Press, 1995); Marcy E. Rosen-

baum and Gun M. Roos, "Women's Experiences of Breast Cancer," in *Breast Cancer: Society Shapes an Epidemic,* ed. Anne S. Kasper and Susan J. Ferguson (New York: Palgrave, 2002); Barbara F. Stevens, *Not Just One in Eight: Stories of Breast Cancer Survivors and Their Families* (Deerfield Beach, Fla.: Health Communications, 2000); Michelle Tocher, *How to Ride a Dragon: Women with Breast Cancer Tell Their Stories* (Toronto: Key Porter Books, 2002). Excellent analyses of this literature include G. Thomas Couser, *Recovering Bodies: Illness, Disability, and Life Writing* (Madison: University of Wisconsin Press, 1997), pp. 36–80; Diane Price Herndl, "Our Breasts, Our Selves: Identity, Community, and Ethics in Cancer Autobiography," *Signs: Journal of Women in Culture and Society,* v. 32, no. 1 (Autumn 2006); Laura Potts, "Publishing the Personal: Autobiographical Narratives of Breast Cancer and the Self," in *Ideologies of Breast Cancer: Feminist Perspectives,* ed. Potts (New York: St. Martin's, 2000), pp. 98–130.

8. Michael J. Hassett, A. James O'Malley, Juliana R. Pakes, Joseph P. Newhouse, and Craig C. Earle, "Frequency and Cost of Chemotherapy-Related Serious Adverse Effects in a Population Sample of Women with Breast Cancer," *Journal of the National Cancer Institute,* v. 98, no. 16 (August 16, 2006): 1108–1117. See also John K. Erban and Joseph Lau, "On the Toxicity of Chemotherapy for Breast Cancer—The Need for Vigilance," *Journal of the National Cancer Institute,* v. 98, no. 16 (August 16, 2006): 1096–1097. The growing involvement of drug companies in medical research may accentuate that bias. As numerous observers note, the pharmaceutical industry tends to minimize adverse drug effects. See, for example, Marcia Angell, *The Truth about the Drug Companies: How They Deceive Us and What to Do about It* (New York: Random House, 2004); Jerry Avorn, *Powerful Medicines: The Benefits, Risks, and Costs of Prescription Drugs* (New York: Vintage Books, 2005). In 2003, the industry was involved in 57 percent of breast cancer studies, up from 44 percent in 1993. (Jeffrey Peppercorn, Emily Blood, Eric Winer, and Ann Partridge, "Association between Pharmaceutical Involvement and Outcomes in Breast Cancer Clinical Trials," *Cancer,* v. 109, no. 7 (April 1, 2007): 1239–1241.

9. See Charles E. Rosenberg, *The Care of Strangers: The Rise of America's Hospital System* (New York: Basic Books, 1987), p. 70.

10. Charles E. Rosenberg, "The Tyranny of Diagnosis: Specific Entities and Individual Experience," *Milbank Quarterly,* v. 80, no. 2 (June 2002): 237–260; Paul Starr, *The Social Transformation of American Medicine: The Rise of a Sovereign Profession and the Making of a Vast Industry* (New York: Basic Books, 1982).

11. See Marcia Meldrum, *The Janus Drugs: Chronic Pain and Drug Control in 21st Century America* (Berkeley: University of California Press, forthcoming).

12. See Rita Charon, *Narrative Medicine: Honoring the Stories of Illness* (New York: Oxford University Press, 2006); Jerome Groopman, *How Doctors Think* (Boston: Houghton Mifflin, 2007).

13. Susan Wendell, "Old Women out of Control: Some Thoughts on Aging, Ethics, and Psychosomatic Medicine," in *Mother Time: Women, Aging, and Ethics*, ed. Margaret Urban Walker (Lanham, Md.: Rowman and Littlefield, 1999), p. 141.

14. Cited in Robert Jay Lifton, *Super Power Syndrome: America's Apocalyptic Confrontation with the World* (New York: Thunder's Mouth Press/Nation Books, 2003), p. 127.

15. See Richard A. Deyo and Donald L. Patrick, *Hope or Hype: The Obsession with Medical Advances and the High Cost of False Promises* (New York: AMACOM, 2005).

16. James T. Patterson, *The Dread Disease: Cancer and Modern American Culture* (Cambridge, Mass.: Harvard University Press, 1987), pp. 22–30. Some scholars, however, argue that the reticence surrounding breast cancer has been greatly exaggerated. See Barbara Clow, "Who's Afraid of Susan Sontag? Or, the Myths and Metaphors of Cancer Reconsidered," *Social History of Medicine*, vol. 14, no. 2 (2001): 293–312; and Kirsten E. Gardner, *Early Detection: Women, Cancer, and Awareness Campaigns in the Twentieth-Century United States* (Chapel Hill: University of North Carolina Press, 2006).

17. Barron H. Lerner, *The Breast Cancer Wars: Fear, Hope, and the Pursuit of a Cure in Twentieth-Century America* (Baltimore: Johns Hopkins University Press, 2001), pp. 15–68.

18. James S. Olson, *Bathsheba's Breast: Women, Cancer, and History* (Baltimore: Johns Hopkins University Press, 2002), pp. 67, 89.

19. Lerner, *Breast Cancer Wars*, p. 142.

20. Ibid.

21. Ibid., pp. 92–140.

22. Gardner, *Early Detection*, pp. 86–88.

23. Terese Lasser, "I Had Breast Cancer," *Coronet* (April 1954): 109.

24. Ibid., pp. 147–151; Lerner, *Breast Cancer Wars*, pp. 142–144.

25. Quoted in Lester David, "A Brave Family Faces Up to Breast Cancer," *Today's Health* (June 1972): 20.

26. Helga Sandburg, "Let a Joy Keep You," *McCall's* (November 1974): 68.

27. Betty Rollin, "The Best Years of My Life," *New York Times Magazine* (February 1980): 36–37.

28. Audre Lorde, *The Cancer Journals* (Argyle, N.H.: Spinsters Ink, 1980), p. 68.

29. Lerner, *Breast Cancer Wars*, p. 193.

30. Jean Zalon and Jean L. Block, *I Am Whole Again: The Case for Breast Reconstruction after Mastectomy* (New York: Random House, 1978), p. 32.

31. Ibid., p. 136.

32. Ibid., pp. 251–252.

33. Ibid., p. 154.

34. See S. Berube, L. Provencher, J. Robert, S. Jacob, N. Hebert-Croteau, J. Lemieux, T. Duchesne, and J. Brisson, "Quantitative Exploration of Possible Reasons for the Recent Improvement in Breast Cancer Survival," *Breast Cancer Research and Treatment*, v. 106, no. 3 (December 2007): 419–431; P. A. Wingo, L. A. Ries, S. L. Parker, and C. W. Heath, Jr., "Long-Term Cancer Patient Survival in the United States," *Cancer Epidemiology, Biomarkers and Prevention*, v. 7, no. 4 (April 1989): 271–282.

35. "Melissa Etheridge Talks about Breast Cancer: Etheridge Sings in 'GMA's' Women Rule Concert Series," ABC News, October 19, 2005.

36. Barbara Ehrenreich, "Welcome to Cancerland," in *The Best American Essays, 2002,* ed. Stephen Jay Gould (Boston: Houghton Mifflin, 2002), p. 87.

37. Ibid., pp. 73–74.

38. All names of the survivors in this study are pseudonyms.

Notes to Chapter I

1. Susan J. Brison, *Aftermath and the Remaking of a Self* (Princeton, N.J.: Princeton University Press, 2002), p. 39.

2. Judith Herman, *Trauma and Recovery* (New York: Basic Books, 1992), p. 57.

3. Ibid.

4. Susan Bolotin, "Slash, Burn and Poison," *New York Times* (April 13, 1997).

5. Ibid., pp. 37–42.

6. It also is possible that the rates are inflated because some women included symptoms experienced either during treatment or the year after it ended, despite our instructions to the contrary.

7. Institute of Medicine and National Research Council, *From Cancer Patient to Cancer Survivor: Lost in Transition* (Washington, D.C.: National Academies Press, 2006).

8. Ibid., p. 75.

9. J. E. Bower, P. A. Ganz, K. A. Desmond, J. H. Rowland, B. E. Meyerowitz, and T. R. Belin, "Fatigue in Breast Cancer Survivors: Occurrence, Correlates, and Impact on Quality of Life," *Journal of Clinical Oncology*, v. 18, no. 4 (2000): 743–853.

10. Daniel H. S. Silverman, Christine J. Dy, Steven A. Castellon, Jasmine Lai, Betty S. Pio, Laura Abraham, Kari Waddell, Laura Peterson, Michael E. Phelps, and Patricia A. Ganz, "Altered Frontocortical, Cerebellar, and Basal Ganglia Activity in Adjuvant-Treated Breast Cancer Survivors 5–10 Years after Chemotherapy," *Breast Cancer Research and Treatment*, v. 103, no. 3 (July 2007): 303–311.

11. See Marilyn Yalom, *A History of the Breast* (New York: Ballantine Books, 1997).

12. Diane Price Herndl, "Our Breasts, Our Selves: Identity, Community, and Ethics in Cancer Autobiography," *Signs: Women in Culture and Society*, v. 32, no. 1 (Autumn 2006): 221.

13. Arthur Kleinman, *The Illness Narratives: Suffering, Healing, and the Human Condition* (New York: Basic Books, 1988), p. 31.

Notes to Chapter 2

1. CMF treatment consists of three chemotherapy drugs: cyclophosphamide, methotrexate, and fluorouracil.

2. PDR is the abbreviation for the *Physicians Desk Reference,* a compilation of information about prescription drugs.

3. HRT is an abbreviation for hormone replacement therapy.

4. See Michael S. Goldstein, "The Persistence and Resurgence of Medical Pluralism," *Journal of Health Politics, Policy and Law*, v. 29, nos. 4–5 (August-October 2004): 925–945; Sydney A. Halpern, "Medical Authority and the Culture of Rights," *Journal of Health Politics, Policy, and Law*, v. 29, nos. 4–5 (August-October 2004): 835–852; Bernice A. Pescosolido and Jack K. Martin, "Cultural Authority and the Sovereignty of American Medicine: The Role of Networks, Class, and Community," *Journal of Health Politics, Policy, and Law*, v. 29, nos. 4–5 (August-October 2004): 735–756; Bernice A. Pescosolido, Steven A. Tuch, and Jack K. Martin, "The Profession of Medicine and the Public: Examining Americans' Changing Confidence in Physician Authority from the Beginning of the 'Health Care Crisis' to the Era of Health Care Reform," *Journal of Health and Social Behavior*, v. 42 (March 2001): 1–16; David J. Rothman, "The Origins and Consequences of Patient Autonomy": A 25-Year

Retrospective," *Health Care Analysis,* v. 9 (2001): 255–264; Keith Wailoo, Timothy Stoltzfus Jost, and Mark Schlesinger, "Professional Sovereignty in a Changing Health Care System: Reflections on Paul Starr's *The Social Transformation of American Medicine,*" *Journal of Health Politics, Policy and Law,* v. 29, nos. 4–5 (August-October 2004): 557–568.

5. See Maren Klawiter, "Breast Cancer in Two Regimes: The Impact of Social Movements on Illness Experience," *Sociology of Health and Illness,* v. 26, no. 6 (2004): 845–874; Ellen Leopold, *In a Darker Ribbon: Breast Cancer, Women, and Their Doctors in the Twentieth Century* (Boston: Beacon, 1999); Barron H. Lerner, *The Breast Cancer Wars: Fear, Hope, and the Pursuit of a Cure in Twentieth-Century America* (New York: Oxford University Press, 2001).

6. Lerner, *Breast Cancer Wars,* 140.

7. See L. Ebony Boulware, Lisa A. Cooper, Lloyd E. Ratner, Thomas A. LaVeist, and Neil R. Powe, "Race and Trust in the Health Care System," *Public Health Reports,* v. 118 (July-August 2004): 358–365.

8. See Vanessa Northington Gamble, "Under the Shadow of Tuskegee: African Americans and Health Care," in *Tuskegee's Truths" Rethinking the Tuskegee Syphilis Study,* ed. Susan M. Reverby (Chapel Hill: University of North Carolina Press, 2000), pp. 431–442.

9. See J. Green-McKenzie, "Training African-American Residents in the Twentieth Century," *Journal of the National Medical Association,*" v. 96, no. 23 (March 2004): 372–375; K. L. Moseley, "After Flexner: The Challenge," *Journal of the National Medical Association,* v. 98, no. 9 (September 2006): 1430–1431.

10. On the preference of African American patients for physicians of the same race, see F. M. Chen, F. R. Fryer, Jr., R. L. Phillips, Jr., E. Wilson, and D. E. Pathman, "Patients' Beliefs about Racism, Preferences for Physician Race, and Satisfaction with Care," *Annals of Family Medicine,* v. 3, no. 2 (March-April 2005): 138–143; T. A. LaVeist and T. Carroll, "Race of Physician and Satisfaction with Care among African-American Patients," *Journal of the National Medical Association,* v. 94, no. 11 (November 2002): 937–943; T. A. LaVeist and A. Nuru-Jeter, "Is Doctor-Patient Race Concordance Associated with Greater Satisfaction with Care?" *Journal of Health and Social Behavior,* v. 43, no. 3 (September 2002): 296–306.

11. Laura A. Siminoff, Gregory C. Graham, and Nahida H. Gordon, "Cancer Communication Patterns and the Influence of Patient Characteristics: Disparities in Information-Giving and Affective Behaviors," *Patient Education and Counseling,* v. 62 (2006): 355–360.

12. Ibid.

13. For another account of breast cancer patients' views of medicine, see Jennifer Fosket, "Problematizing Biomedicine: Women's Constructions of Breast Cancer Knowledge," in *Ideologies of Breast Cancer: Feminist Perspectives*, ed. Laura K. Potts (New York: St. Martin's, 2000), pp. 15–36.

14. See A. S. Elstein, "Clinical Reasoning in Medicine," in *Clinical Reasoning in the Health Professions*, ed. J. Higgs and M. A. Jones (Woburn, Mass.: Butterworth-Heinemann, 1995), pp. 49–59; Jerome Groopman, *How Doctors Think* (Boston: Houghton Mifflin, 2007), p. 276.

15. See Groopman, *How Doctors Think*, pp. 187–188.

16. Gina Kolata with Melody Peterson, "Hormone Replacement Study a Shock to the Medical System," *New York Times* (July 10, 2002): A1, A16; Elizabeth Siegel Watkins, *The Estrogen Elixir: A History of Hormone Replacement Therapy in America* (Baltimore: Johns Hopkins University Press, 2007); Feifei Wei, Diana L. Miglioretti, Maureen T. Connelly, et al., "Changes in Women's Use of Hormones after the Women's Health Initiative Estrogen and Progestin Trial by Race, Education, and Income," *Journal of the National Cancer Institute Monographs*, v. 35 (2005): 106–112.

17. JoAnn E. Manson et al., "Estrogen Therapy and Coronary-Artery Calcification," *New England Journal of Medicine* (June 21, 2007): 2591–2602; Thomas H. Maugh II, "Doctors Change Course Again on Estrogen Therapy," *Los Angeles Times* (June 21, 2007): A1.

18. See Watkins, *Estrogen Elixir*.

19. For evidence that physicians' gender shapes relationships with patients, see Debra L. Roter and Judith Hall, *Doctors Talking with Patients/Patients Talking with Doctors: Improving Communication in Medical Visits*, 2nd ed. (Westport, Conn.: Praeger, 2006): 95–106.

20. See Klawiter, "Breast Cancer in Two Regimes."

21. Derjung Tarn, John Heritage, Debora A. Paternitti, Ron D. Hays, Richard L. Kravitz, and Neil S. Wenger, "Physician Communication When Prescribing New Medications," *Archives in Internal Medicine*, v. 166 (September 25, 2006): 1835–1862.

22. See Groopman, *How Doctors Think*, p. 19.

23. Susan Wendell, *The Rejected Body: Feminist Philosophical Reflections on Disability* (New York: Routledge, 1996), p. 122.

24. Deborah A. Stone, *The Disabled State* (Philadelphia: Temple University Press, 1984), p. 4.

25. On the ability of support groups to bolster patients' trust in their own knowledge, see Mark A. Chesler, "Mobilizing Consumer Activism in Health Care: The Role of Self-Help Groups," *Research in Social Movements: Conflicts and*

Change, v. 13 (1991): 275–305; Steven Epstein, *Impure Science: AIDS, Activism, and the Politics of Knowledge* (Berkeley: University of California Press, 2006), pp. 9–10; Miriam J. Steward, "Expanding Theoretical Conceptualizations of Self-Help Groups," *Social Science and Medicine,* v. 31 (May 1990): 1057–1066; also see special issue of the *American Journal of Community Psychology,* v. 19 (October 1991).

26. See Robert A. Aronowitz, "From Myalgic Encephalitis to Yuppie Flu: A History of Chronic Fatigue Syndromes," in *Framing Disease: Studies in Cultural History,* ed. Charles E. Rosenberg and Janet Golden (New Brunswick, N.J.: Rutgers University Press, 1992), pp. 155–181; Lesley Cooper, "Myalgic Encephalomyelitis and the Medical Encounter," *Sociology of Health and Illness,* v. 19, no. 2 (1997): 186–207.

27. Roni Caryn Rabin, "A Painful Lymph Illness Often Follows Cancer," *New York Times* (June 5, 2007).

28. See Paula Kamen, *All in My Head: An Epic Quest to Cure an Unrelenting, Totally Unreasonable, and Only Slightly Enlightening Headache* (Cambridge, Mass.: Da Capo, 2005), p. 14.

29. Elliot G. Mishler, *The Discourse of Medicine: Dialectics of Medical Interviews* (Norwood, N.J.: Ablex, 1984).

30. In her wide-ranging diatribe against the current breast cancer movement, Barbara Ehrenreich dismisses support groups as the handmaidens of the medical establishment. Noting that "no one leaves the hospital without a brochure directing her to local support groups," Ehrenreich concludes they have "won the stamp of medical approval" because "they are no longer perceived as seditious." By way of contrast, she points to the more "ideological" self-help groups that formed the organizing tool of the women's health movement in the seventies and eighties. (Barbara Ehrenreich, "Welcome to Cancerland," in *The Best American Essays, 2002,* ed. Stephen Jay Gould [Boston: Houghton Mifflin, 2002], p. 74.) But those two types of groups may be more alike than she imagines. Even patients who enter support groups at a hospital's behest may discover themselves forging an oppositional stance. The members of Pat Garland's group helped to hone her anger at the doctors she encountered.

31. Institute of Medicine and National Research Council, *From Cancer Patient to Survivor: Lost in Transition* (Washington, D.C.: National Academies Press, 2006), pp. 192–197. Although the statement about the focus of follow-up services is based on a British study, the report notes that "anecdotal evidence" suggests that the "same pattern of care" exists in the United States (ibid., p. 197).

32. Epstein, *Impure Science,* p. 23.

Notes to Chapter 3

1. David M. Eisenberg, Roger B. Davis, Susan L. Ettner, Scott Appel, Sonja Wilkey, Maria Van Rompay, and Ronald C. Kessler, "Trends in Alternative Medicine Use in the United States, 1990–1997: Results of a Follow-Up National Study," *JAMA*, v. 280, no. 18 (November 11, 1998): 1569–1575. Although we asked women whether they had used nontraditional therapies to address their symptoms, we did not specify that the use had to have occurred within the past year. As a result, our sample cannot be directly compared to Eisenberg's respondents.

2. John A. Astin, "Why Patients Use Alternative Medicine: Results of a National Study," *JAMA*, v. 279, no. 19 (May 20, 1998): 1551; Eisenberg et al., "Trends in Alternative Medicine Use," p. 1571.

3. Astin, "Why Patients Use Alternative Medicine," p. 1550.

4. See Michael S. Goldstein, "The Persistence and Resurgence of Medical Pluralism," *Journal of Health Politics, Policy and Law*, v. 29, nos. 4–5 (August-October 2004): 129.

5. For an analysis of the core beliefs distinguishing alternative medicine from conventional health care, see Michael S. Goldstein, *Alternative Health Care: Medicine, Miracle, or Mirage?* (Philadelphia: Temple University Press, 1999), pp. 40–73.

6. See "When Trust in Doctors Erodes, Other Treatments Fill the Void," *New York Times* (February 3, 2006): A1, A20.

7. Eisenberg et al., "Trends in Alternative Medicine Use," p. 1573.

8. Astin, "Why Patients Use Alternative Medicine," p. 1551.

9. See Roni Caryn Rabin, "A Painful Lymph Illness Often Follows Cancer," *New York Times* (June 5, 2007).

10. Erving Goffman, *Stigma: Notes on the Management of Spoiled Identity* (New York: Simon and Schuster, 1963), pp. 73–91.

11. See Kirsten E. Gardner, *Early Detection: Women, Cancer, and Awareness Campaigns in the Twentieth-Century United States* (Chapel Hill: University of North Carolina Press, 2006).

12. Audre Lorde, *The Cancer Journals* (San Francisco: Spinsters Ink, 1980), p. 59.

13. Sharon Batt, "'Perfect People': Cancer Charities," in *The Politics of Women's Bodies: Sexuality, Appearance, and Behavior,* ed. Rose Weitz (New York: Oxford University Press, 1998), p. 146.

14. Susan J. Brison, *Aftermath: Violence and the Remaking of a Self* (Princeton, N.J.: Princeton University Press, 2002), p. 73.

15. Kathy Charmaz, *Good Days, Bad Days: The Self in Chronic Illness and Times* (New Brunswick, N.J.: Rutgers University Press, 1991), p. 122.

16. Gina Kolata, "The Body Heretic: It Scorns Our Efforts," *New York Times Week in Review* (April 17, 2005), 1.

Notes to Chapter 4

1. Judith Herman, *Trauma and Recovery: The Aftermath of Violence—from Domestic Abuse to Political Terror* (New York: Basic Books, 1992), p. 61.

2. See Kathy Charmaz, *Good Days, Bad Days: The Self in Illness and Time* (New Brunswick, N.J.: Rutgers University Press, 1991).

3. See Ann Crittenden, *The Price of Motherhood: Why the Most Important Job in the World Is Still the Least Valued* (New York: Metropolitan Books, 2001); Joan Williams, *Unbending Gender: Why Family and Work Conflict and What to Do about It* (New York: Oxford University Press, 2000).

4. This is a very common response. See C. Dunkel-Schetter and C. B. Wortman, "The Interpersonal Dynamics of Cancer: Problems in Social Relationships and Their Impact on the Patient," in *Interpersonal Issues in Health Care*, ed. H. S. Friedman and M. R. DiMatteo (New York: Academic Press, 1982), pp. 69–100.

5. For information about children's responses to their mothers' breast cancer, see B. A. Hilton and H. Elfert, "Children's Experiences with Mothers' Early Breast Cancer," *Cancer Practice*, v. 4, no. 2 (March-April 1996): 96–104; G. Forrest, C. Plumb, S. Ziebland, and A. Stein, "Breast Cancer in the Family—Children's Perceptions of Their Mother's Cancer and Its Initial Treatment: Qualitative Study," *British Medical Journal* (April 29, 2006): 998–1003; E. H. Zahlis, "The Child's Worries about the Mother's Breast Cancer: Sources of Distress in School-Age Children," *Oncology Nursing Forum*, v. 28, no. 6 (July 2001): 1019–1025.

6. *Los Angeles Breast Health Resource Guide*, 5th ed. (Los Angeles: Los Angeles County Regional Cancer Detection Partnership, n.d.), 69–73. Some offer multiple groups; some also furnish separate services for African American, Chinese, Japanese, Korean, Latina, Native American, and lesbian women.

7. See Margaret H. Vickers, "The 'Invisibly' Chronically Ill as Unexamined Organizational Fringe-Dwellers: Voices of Ambiguity, Confusion, and Uncertainty," *Sociology of Work*, v. 9 (2000): 3–21.

8. See Julia Lawton, "Lay Experiences in Health and Illness: Past Research and Future Agendas," *Sociology of Health and Illness*, v. 25 (Silver Anniversary Issue 2003): 23–40.

Notes to Chapter 5

1. Institute of Medicine and National Research Council, *From Cancer Patient to Cancer Survivor: Lost in Transition* (Washington, D.C.: National Academies Press, 2006), p. 367.

2. See Melissa Harris-Lacewell, "No Place to Rest: African American Political Attitudes and the Myth of Black Women's Strength," *Women and Politics*, v. 23, no. 3 (2001): 1–33.

3. See H. Bosma, M. G. Marmot, H. Hemingway, A. C. Nicholson, E. Brunner, and S. A. Stansfeld, "Low Job Control and Risk of Coronary Heart Disease in Whitehall II (Prospective Cohort) Study," *British Medical Journal*, v. 314 (February 22, 1997): 558–565; S. Cohen, W. J. Doyle, and A. Baum, "Socioeconomic Status Is Association with Stress Hormones," *Psychosomatic Medicine*, v. 68, no. 3 (May–June 2006): 414–420; H. Kuper and M. Marmot, "Job Strain, Job Demands, Decision Latitude, and Risk of Coronary Heart Disease within the Whitehall II Study," *Journal of Epidemiological Community Health*, v. 57, no. 2 (February 2003): 147–153; A. Steptoe, S. Kunz-Ebrecht, N. Owen, P. J. Feldman, G. Willemsen, C. Kirschbaum, and M. Marmot, "Socioeconomic Status and Stress-Related Biological Responses over the Working Day," *Psychosomatic Medicine*, v. 65, no. 3 (May–June 2003): 461–470.

4. See D. V. Ah, D. H. Kang, and J. S. Carpenter, "Stress, Optimism, and Social Support: Impact on Immune Responses in Breast Cancer," *Research in Nursing and Health*, v. 30, no. 1 (February 2007): 72–83; B. L. Andersen, W. B. Farrar, D. Golden-Kreutz, L. A. Kutz, R. MacCallum, M. E. Courtney, and R. Glaser, "Stress and Immune Responses after Surgical Treatment for Regional Breast Cancer," *Journal of the National Cancer Institute*, v. 90, no. 1 (January 7, 1998): 30–36.

5. See Ruth O'Brien, *Crippled Justice: The History of Modern Disability Policy in the Workplace* (Chicago: University of Chicago Press, 2001), p. 177.

6. See John Leland, "When Even Health Insurance Is No Safeguard," *New York Times* (October 23, 2005): 1, 24.

7. See Institute of Medicine and National Research Council, *From Cancer Patient to Cancer Survivor*, p. 391.

Notes to Chapter 6

1. Arthur W. Frank, *The Wounded Storyteller: Body, Illness, and Ethics* (Chicago: University of Chicago Press, 1995), p. 115.

2. Anne Hunsaker Hawkins, "A Change of Heart: The Paradigm of Regeneration in Medical and Religious Narrative," *Perspectives in Biology and Medicine*, v. 33, no. 4 (Summer 1990): 556.

3. Daniel J. Wilson, "Covenants of Work and Grace: Themes of Recovery and Redemption in Polio Narratives," *Literature and Medicine*, v. 13, no. 1 (Spring 1994): 22–41.

4. Diane Price Herndl, "Our Breasts, Our Selves: Identity, Community, and Ethics in Cancer Autobiographies," *Signs: Journal of Women in Culture and Society*, v. 32, no. 1 (Autumn 2006): 224. Herndl draws primarily on four books: *Breast Cancer? Let Me Check My Schedule*, ed. Peggy McCarthy and Jo An Loren (Boulder, Colo.: Westview, 1997); *The Breast Cancer Book of Strength and Courage: Inspiring Stories to See You through Your Journey*, ed. Judie Fertig Panneton and Ernie Bodai (Roseville, Calif.: Prima, 2002); Rita Busch, Judy Thibault Klevins, Daena Kluegel, Jana Morgana, Helen Rash, Katherine Traynham, and Lesley Tyson, *Can You Come Here Where I Am? The Poetry and Prose of Seven Breast Cancer Survivors* (Manassas, Va.: E. M. Press, 1998); Hilda Raz, *Living on the Margins: Women Writers on Breast Cancer* (New York: Persea, 1999).

5. Barbara Ehrenreich, "Welcome to Cancerland," in *The Best American Essays, 2002*, ed. Stephen Jay Gould (Boston: Houghton Mifflin, 2002), p. 78.

6. Kathlyn Conway, *Ordinary Life: A Memoir of Illness* (New York: W. H. Freeman, 1997), p. 1.

7. Frank argues that an essential feature of the "quest narrative" is the development of a "communicative body," which "constructs its humanity in relation to other bodies" (Frank, *Wounded Storyteller*, p. 49). That argument, however, rests on the assumption that the ill person previously had been relatively detached from others and thus probably accords better with men's experiences than with women's. The end result of the "quests" of many women we interviewed was separation rather than attachment.

8. In his memoir of life after severe brain damage, writer Floyd Skloot similarly reflects on the benefits of savoring the present: "I have come to pay tremendous value on the intensity and power of the moment." *In the Shadow of Memory* (Lincoln: University of Nebraska Press, 2003), p. 41.

9. See B. A. Brenner, "Sister Support: Women Create a Breast Cancer Movement," in *Breast Cancer: Society Shapes an Epidemic*, ed. A. S. Kasper and S. J. Ferguson (New York: St. Martin's, 2000); Maren Klawiter, "Breast Cancer in Two Regimes: The Impact of Social Movements on Illness Experience," *Sociology of Health and Illness*, v. 26, no. 6 (2004): 845–874; Jennifer R. Myhre, "The Breast Cancer Movement: Seeing beyond Consumer Activism,"

Journal of the American Medical Women's Association, v. 54, no. 1 (Winter 1999): 29–33; National Breast Cancer Coalition website, www.natlbcc.org.

10. The literature on black women and breast cancer is extensive. Selected studies include A. Ghafoor, A. Jemal, E. Ward, V. Cokkinides, R. Smith, and M. Thun, "Trends in Breast Cancer by Race and Ethnicity," *CA: A Cancer Journal for Clinicians,* v. 54, no. 3 (2003): 3422–3455; I. Jatoi, H. Becher, and C. R. Leake, "Widening Disparity in Survival between White and African-American Patients with Breast Carcinoma Treated in the U.S. Department of Defense Healthcare System," *Cancer,* v. 98, no. 5 (September 1, 2003): 894–899; S. A. Joslyn and M. M. West, "Racial Differences in Breast Carcinoma Survival," *Cancer,* v. 88, no. 1 (January 1, 2000): 114–123; Donald R. Lannin, Holly F. Matthews, Jim Mitchell, Melvin S. Swanson, Frances H. Swanson, and Maxine S. Edwards, "Influence of Socioeconomic and Cultural Factors on Racial Differences in Late-Stage Presentation of Breast Cancer," *Journal of the American Medical Association,* v. 279 (1998): 1801–1807; E. T. Johnson, "Breast Cancer Racial Differences before Age Forty—Implications for Screening," *Journal of the National Medical Association,* v. 94, no. 3 (March 2002): 149–156; M. Sarker, I. Jatoi, and H. Becher, "Racial Differences in Breast Cancer Survival in Women under Age Sixty," *Breast Cancer Research and Treatment,* v. 106, no. 1 (November 2007): 135–141.

11. Cited in Frank, *Wounded Storyteller,* p. 35.

12. The phrase is James T. Patterson's in *The Dread Disease: Cancer and Modern American Culture* (Cambridge, Mass.: Harvard University Press, 1987), p. 13.

Notes to the Conclusion

1. Rita Charon, *Narrative Medicine: Honoring the Stories of Illness* (New York: Oxford University Press, 2006), p. 65.

2. Jane Gross, "Chemotherapy Fog Is No Longer Ignored as Illusion," *New York Times* (April 29, 2007), p. 1.

3. See, e.g., Julie K. Silver, *After Cancer Treatment: Heal Faster, Better, Stronger* (Baltimore: Johns Hopkins University Press, 2006).

4. See John E. Robison, Laurent Perreard, and Philip S. Bernard, "State of the Science: Molecular Classifications of Breast Cancer for Clinical Diagnostics," *Clinical Biochemistry,* v. 37 (2004): 572–578.

5. See J. A. Sparano, "TAILORx: Trial Assigning Individualized Options for Treatment (Rx)," *Clinical Breast Cancer,* v. 7, no. 4 (October 2006): 347–350.

6. See Kim Irwin, "Living after Cancer," *UCLA Medicine* (Winter 2007): 12–17.

7. Jerome Groopman, *How Doctors Think* (Boston: Houghton Mifflin, 2007), pp. 1–26.

8. Robert A. Aronowitz, *Making Sense of Illness: Science, Society, and Disease* (Cambridge: Cambridge University Press, 1998), p. 175.

9. Groopman, *How Doctors Think*, p. 6.

10. See William T. Branch, David Kern, Paul Haidet, Peter Weissmann, Catherine F. Gracey, Gary Mitchell, and Thomas Inui, "Teaching the Human Dimensions of Care in Clinical Settings," *Journal of the American Medical Association*, v. 286, no. 9 (September 5, 2001): 1067–1074.

11. See Marguerite Holloway, "When Medicine Meets Literature," *ScientificAmerican.com* (April 25, 2005).

12. See Simi Linton, *Claiming Disability: Knowledge and Identity* (New York: New York University Press, 1998); Paul K. Longmore, *Why I Burned My Book and Other Essays on Disability* (Philadelphia: Temple University Press, 2003); Rosemarie Garland Thomson, *Extraordinary Bodies: Figuring Physical Disability in American Culture and Literature* (New York: Columbia University Press, 1997).

13. See Rick Baldoz, Charles Koeber, and Philip Kraft, "Making Sense of Work in the Twenty-First Century," in *The Critical Study of Work: Labor, Technology, and Global Production*, ed. Rick Baldoz, Charles Koeber, and Philip Kraft (Philadelphia: Temple University Press, 2001); Juliet B. Schor, *The Overworked American: The Unexpected Decline of Leisure* (New York: Basic Books, 1991).

14. See Rosemarie Garland-Thomson, "Feminist Disability Studies," *Signs: Journal of Women in Culture and Society*, v. 30, no. 2 (2005). See also Erving Goffman, *Stigma: Notes on the Management of Spoiled Identity* (New York: Simon and Schuster, 1963).

Index

acceptance, 78–80, 117, 121

acupuncture, 68

Adriamycin, 27–28, 52, 103

African American women: attitudes toward alternative therapies, 71–72; death rates from breast cancer, 134–135; interviews of, 149–150; posttreatment symptoms as another trouble to bear, 12; spiritual awakenings, 125; work, 103–104

aging, feelings of, 22–23

alternative therapies, 65–80; acupuncture, 68; African American women's attitudes toward, 71–72; avoidance of, 70; biofeedback, 68; Briggs's use of, 72; chiropractic, 68; concerns about, 70; coordination with conventional therapies, 70–71; cost of, 70; definition, 67; dissatisfaction with conventional medicine, 69; energy healing, 68; fragmentation of care, 70; herbal medicine, 68; holistic medicine, 65; homeopathy, 68; hypnosis, 68; massage, 68, 70; McKnight's use of, 68–69, 71; quality of, 70; race-based referrals, 72; racial differences in attitudes toward, 71–72; Thom-

as's use of, 65–67, 147; Trawick's use of, 69; usage rates, 67–68, 162n1; white women's attitudes toward, 71–72; yoga, 147

American Association of Medical Colleges, 141

American Cancer Society: campaign against "conspiracy of silence," 137; encouragement of early detection, 7; "Look Good, Feel Good" program, 74–75; Reach to Recovery program, 8, 74, 146; volunteer work for, 91, 135, 147

American Cancer Society for the Control of Cancer, 7

Americans with Disabilities Act (ADA), 110

antidepressants, 60

anxiety, 22, 27, 29, 33

aromatase inhibitors, xi

Aronowitz, Robert, 140

arthritis, 14, 27

Avon Corporation, 117

Barlow, Marge (survivor, pseudonym), 10–11, 119–122, 143–144; acceptance of contingency and change, 121; altered sense of time, 120, 129; anxiety, 33; cognitive impairment, 11, 54;

About the Authors

EMILY ABEL is Professor in both the Women's Studies Department and the School of Public Health at UCLA.

SASKIA SUBRAMANIAN is Assistant Research Sociologist at the UCLA Center for Culture and Health, Department of Psychiatry and Biobehavioral Studies.

CPSIA information can be obtained
at www.ICGtesting.com
Printed in the USA
BVHW030926060319
541928BV00001B/2/P